21

21 Picador Authors Celebrate

21

TARIQ ALI
JULIAN BARNES
JIM CRACE
RUSSELL HOBAN
CHRISTOPHER HOPE
CLIVE JAMES
TAMA JANOWITZ
MARK LAWSON
KATHY LETTE
NORMAN LEWIS
PATRICK McCABE
IAN McEWAN
ROBERT McLIAM WILSON
CANDIA McWILLIAM
CHARLES NICHOLL
CARYL PHILLIPS
DAVID PROFUMO
OLIVER SACKS
GRAHAM SWIFT
COLM TÓIBÍN
EDMUND WHITE

21 Years of International Writing

PICADOR

First published 1993 by Pan Books Limited

a division of Pan Macmillan Publishers Limited
Cavaye Place London SW10 9PG
and Basingstoke

Associated companies throughout the world

ISBN 0 330 33131 0 (Hardback)
ISBN 0 330 33132 9 (Paperback)

Some of the material of 'Pope in Ugandan Discussions'
appeared, in a different form, in a talk for *Joining the Cubs*,
a BBC Radio 4 series, broadcast in 1991.

1 3 5 7 9 8 6 4 2

A CIP catalogue record for this book is available from
the British Library

Typeset by Cambridge Composing (UK) Limited, Cambridge
Printed by Mackays of Chatham PLC, Kent

CONTENTS

OLIVER SACKS

1972

37 Mapesbury Road in North London.
The house where Oliver Sacks was born and grew up,
drawn by Stephen Wiltshire

As ONE grows older the years seem to blur into one another, but 1972 remains sharply etched in my memory. Nineteen sixty-nine had been a year of overwhelming intensity, with the 'awakenings', the tribulations, then the accommodations, of my post-encephalitic patients – such an experience is not given to one twice in a lifetime. Nor, usually, even once. Its preciousness and depth, its intensity and range, made me feel I had to articulate it somehow, but I could not imagine an appropriate form, one which could combine the objectivity of science with the intense sense of fellow-feeling, the closeness with my patients I had, and the sheer wonder at it all.

I had got to know Auden a bit in this year, and he had visited Mount Carmel and seen some of my patients; he wrote about this in 'Old People's Home'. He too felt I would have to transcend medical writing, to find some radically new and very personal form; and that I might need also to find a 'philosophy' to help organize my thoughts.

The experience continued, torrentially, through 1970 and 1971, but a form, a way of articulating it, continued to evade me. I entered 1972, then, with a sharp sense of frustration, an uncertainty as to whether I would ever find a way of binding the experience, and forging it into some organic unity and form.

In Easter of 1972 I discovered Leibniz, discovered him with the force of revelation. I had previously been stuck with a dry, Humean scepticism, which seemed to deny life, or will, or creativity, or identity. In Leibniz (in words which could have been written in fire!) I found, or imagined I had found, the complete opposite – an affirmation of life, and will, and identity, and their grounding and validation in a coherent philosophy. Reading Leibniz, I had a sense of coming home, after twenty years or more of alienation and desiccation.

I still regarded England as my home then (and could regard my twelve years in the States as little more than a prolonged visit) – it was where I was born, where I had spent the first twenty-seven years of my life. It seemed to me that I needed to return, to go home to write. 'Home' meant many things – the huge, rambling house in Mapesbury Road where I was born, and where my parents, now in their seventies, still lived; but equally Hampstead Heath, which we loved to walk to, and where I used to play, endlessly, as a child.

In '72, then, I decided to take the summer off, and to get myself a flat on the edge of Hampstead Heath, within easy range of the walks, the mushroomed woods, the swimming ponds I loved, and equally easy range of 'home', '37'. This was an especially good time to return home, for my parents were celebrating their golden wedding anniversary in June, and there would be a gathering of the families – my mother being the sixteenth of eighteen children, the cousinhood, in its generations, now numbered in the hundreds – I had always thought of us as a clan or a tribe. But I had a more specific reason for being close: my mother, a surgeon, but trained in neurology, was herself a natural storyteller. She would not only tell medical stories to her colleagues, her students, her patients, her friends, she would enchant the grocer and the milkman by the hour when they came to the door, and she would tell us – my three brothers and me – medical stories from our earliest days, stories sometimes grim and terrifying, but always evocative of the personal qualities, the special value and valour, of the patient. Indeed, the entire atmosphere of the house was one of medical stories – my father too was a grand medical storyteller – and my parents' sense of wonder at the vagaries of life, their combination of a clinical and a narrative cast of mind, was transmitted with great force to all of us. My own impulse to write – not to write fiction or poems, but to chronicle and describe – seems to me to have come directly from them.

My mother had been fascinated when I told her of my patients' 'awakenings'. She kept asking for more and more details, and with the power of her own imagination and sympathy she got to know them, feel for them, as intensely as I did. Rose R. (later to become 'Deborah' in Pinter's play *A Kind of Alaska*) was the one she felt for most deeply. 'You must write their stories,' my mother had been saying since '69, and in 1972 she said, 'Now! This is the time.'

5

In the summer of '72, then, I spent each morning walking and swimming on the Heath, each afternoon writing or dictating the stories of *Awakenings*, and every evening I would stroll down Frognal to Mill Lane, and then to Mapesbury Road, to the rambling old corner house at 37, where I would read the latest instalment to my mother. She had read to me, by the hour, when I was a child – I first experienced Dickens, Trollope, D. H. Lawrence, through her reading – and now she wanted me to read to her, to give written form to the stories she already knew so well. She would listen intently, always with emotion, but always, equally, with a sharp critical judgement, one honed on her own sense of the real. She tolerated, with mixed feelings, my meanderings and ponderings, but 'ringing true' was her ultimate value. 'That doesn't ring true!' she would sometimes say, angrily, but then, more and more, 'Now you have it. Now it rings true.'

In a sort of way, then, we wrote *Awakenings* (at least its stories) together that summer, and there was a sense of time arrested, of enchantment, a privileged time out from the rush of daily life, a special time consecrated to creation – and I dreaded its end, the fall, my return to New York.

It was now past Labor Day, America was back at work – and I too had to return to the daily grind. I did so with an odd sense of foreboding and dread, though why I should have had this, neither I nor my analyst could discern. Towards the end of October my parents went on a trip to Israel, where they had been invited to a medical meeting in the Negev. My mother, especially, did not want to go, but wanted to enjoy the Indian summer in England.

On 13 November, my brother David phoned me from England – our mother had had a heart attack, had just died in Israel. I took the next plane to England, and with my brothers carried her coffin at the funeral. I had wondered how I would feel about sitting shiva, the seven days of ritual mourning prescribed by Jewish law. I did not know if I could bear it, sitting all day on a low stool with my fellow mourners, for seven days on end, receiving a constant stream of people, and talking, talking, talking endlessly, of the departed. But I found this a deep and crucial and affirmative experience, this total sharing of emotions and memories, when, alone, I felt so annihilated by my mother's death.

It especially moved me to see dozens of her patients and students, and how they talked so vividly and humorously and affectionately of her – to see her through their eyes, as physician and teacher and story-teller. As they spoke of her, I was reminded of my own identity as a physician, teacher, and storyteller, and how this had brought us closer, added a new dimension to our relationship, over the years. It made me feel too that I must complete *Awakenings*, in some sense (at least for myself) as a last tribute to her. A strange sense of peace and sobriety, and of what really mattered, grew stronger and stronger in me with each day of the mourning, a sense of the allegorical dimension of life and death. I found it impossible to read anything mundane at the time – I read the Bible, or Donne's *Devotions*, when I finally went to bed each night. And the Donne seemed to have an almost mystical correspondence with my feelings and *Awakenings* at this time.

When the formal mourning was over, I immediately returned to writing, with a sense of my mother's life and death, and Donne's *Devotions*, dominating all my thoughts. And in this mood, in another week, I wrote the later, more allegorical sections of *Awakenings*, with a feeling, a voice I had never known before. With the death of my mother, and the completion of *Awakenings*, I felt that a chapter of my life had come to an end. Nothing has been too real for me since.

PATRICK McCABE

1973

Confessions of an Irish Acid-Eater

Photo: D. Ellis/Redferns

'Cum on Feel the Noize'

NINETEEN SEVENTY-THREE started off badly for me when I fell in love with a girl from Cavan and started writing all these poems to her and posting them but unfortunately never getting any replies. By the time I had sent her eighty or ninety letters I decided it was time to take the bull by the horns and get the bus to Cavan Town, which is about twenty miles from where I lived at the time. I thought I had a massive search on my hands but would you believe it I ran her to earth in the Central Café where she was sitting with a few of her friends under a poster of Brian Connolly and Sweet, smoking fags. I said to her: 'Can we talk?' and she said: 'We can surely' and waited for me to say something but I started to stutter and couldn't think of anything which in the end led me to blurt out: 'What about us?' When I said that they all started nudging each other. Next thing what does Marion (that was her name) say only: 'What *about* us?' I was dumbfounded. Just at that moment 'I'm The Leader Of The Gang (I Am)' by Gary Glitter came on the jukebox and when I said: 'You know – *us*!' she didn't hear me and cupped her hand over her ear and said: 'What did you say?' I was on the verge of saying: 'Don't do this, Marion. Don't let it end like this.' But I could see by the way she was looking at me that it was all over. With my eyes I said goodbye and went out into the grey Cavan rain. I knew Rob Strong and the Plattermen, my favourite band, a sort of cross between Osibisa and Chicago only better than the pair of them put together, were playing in the Sports Centre so I decided I would stay around for that. That night as luck would have it I met another girl and bought her a Fanta orange. I told her that I thought she looked very pretty and would really like it if she would be my girlfriend. When she didn't say yes on the spot I got as red as a beetroot and the sound of her chewing gum was like thunder in my ears. I was terrified that we were going to just sit there in silence and I would have no option but to watch it all die right there in front of me. But just then Rob went down on his knees and rattled a handful of gravel in his throat and asked us all: 'How many of you like Led Zeppelin, people of Cavan? Hands up all who like Led Zeppelin!' I shot my hand right up and cried: 'Me!' I thought she was going to do it too but she just sat there and went on blowing through the straw into the bottle and asking me for fags. I think I must have given her about fifty altogether. To make a long story short, when the band were playing the national anthem I asked her where she lived and she said: 'Main Street.' I was delighted because unlike a lot of the other streets in Cavan, I knew where that was so obviously I was over the moon except that when I asked her could I leave her home she said: 'No.'

So that ended my two love affairs in Cavan that night and on top of that I got stuck in Butlersbridge on the way home and didn't get in until six o'clock. My mother shouted from the bedroom: 'Where were you?' and when I said: 'Cavan,' she rasped: 'A right-looking head on you chasing women in Cavan where they'd lift the coat off your back.' I didn't know whether that was true or not. And I didn't want to know. All I wanted to do was fall into a deep sleep and with a bit of luck never come to again.

But as a man who is well versed in these matters, Mr Samuel Beckett, has been known to observe, you always do don't you and not long after that I was called to teacher training and before I took my leave for ever, I decided I would have one last go at making it work between Marion and me. I had a very good book called *Complete Lyrics and Drawings* by Bob Dylan. I couldn't make up my mind which one to send but in the end I plumped for: 'My love she speaks like silence/Without ideals or violence/She doesn't have to say she's faithful/ Yet she's true, like ice, like fire.'

On average it took a letter two days to reach Cavan so I reckoned I ought to have a reply by the weekend. Our song of that time was 'Cum On Feel The Noize' by Slade and while I waited in the café I played it about 200 or perhaps 250 times. They said to me: 'What has you so dying-looking sitting there saying nothing?' I didn't say anything just sat there sucking a cigarette wondering maybe did I have tuberculosis or something like that. When I wasn't thinking about Marion and our first night together at Threemilehouse carnival I took out my little John Keats book with the gold-embossed binding and read a few snatches of 'La Belle Dame Sans Merci'. It reminded me of her especially when she was in one of her quiet moods. By the end of the week I was beginning to get a bit on edge. But I needn't have worried – Benny Maguire the postman stopped me on the Saturday morning and said: 'I have a letter for you here from Cavan.'

I should have waited until I got home to open it but it's all very wise saying that now – the fact is I couldn't help myself. If anyone had been there looking in over Armstrong's hedge they would have thought I was some kind of madman on the loose with bits of paper flying everywhere. 'Oh, Marion!' I said and there was such a pang of yearning in my stomach I just can't describe it. That was what made it all the more painful for me when I saw the words: 'Stop writing me letters I am going with Francie Melia he's in the army.'

I didn't care if I lived or died after that and to this day I think Marion's treatment of me may have led to my going on drugs or if it didn't it certainly was a contributory factor. They all started saying to me: 'You're not yourself' and I'd say 'So?' which more or less proved their point. And when they said: 'Who do you think Carly Simon's "You're So Vain" is about – Mick Jagger or Warren Beatty?' I'd say: 'I couldn't care less if it's about Donald Duck.' It is a tribute to my friends that despite those difficult times we remain loyal to this day. Particularly in the light of my subsequent behaviour, which was even worse. Some months later, now seeing myself as a part of Dublin's twilight narcotics world, it was only with the greatest of reluctance I spoke to them or answered their questions at all. When they'd praise Gilbert O'Sullivan or The Osmonds' latest hit, my lip would curl in a derisive sneer and I'd mutter something about Van Der Graaf Generator or Tonto's Expanding Headband. I remember in fact exploding with laughter when they sheepishly enquired as to whether I might be able to get them 'some stuff'?

But if I thought I was smart I was soon to learn my lesson, and the words of my own mother would come back to haunt me, for what she had said to me that fateful day when I left home was: 'Good luck now, son, mind your prayers and for God's sake stay away from bad company.' By which she meant, as I realize only too well now, the likes of none other than the person who had within days drawn me into his web and who shall be called Dr X just in case of libel. He carried a little silver box his grandmother had given him and which had once contained a beautiful mother-of-pearl rosary presented to her at the Eucharistic Congress of 1932 by Count John McCormack but which was now packed to the lid with lots of little microdot tabs of acid of all hues and colours. By assisting him with the selling of these throughout the hostelries of the capital I found myself entitled to limitless supplies and also trips to zoos, cinemas, graveyards, and anywhere else our expanding heads decided to take us. What bliss it was to be alive during those balmy days of '73, talking to floorboards and staring at little bits of your hand getting up and moving around. It was only when May finally came around and someone said: 'I haven't read all the modern novels on the course yet' that I remembered why I had come to the training college and that I hadn't bought any books not to mention read any. All of a sudden I was seized by a blind panic but by then it was too late. In answer to the question: 'What is your opinion of the use of coincidence in the writing of Thomas Hardy's *Tess of the D'Urbervilles*?' I could only think of one thing to put down and that was: 'I don't have any opinion of it as yet.' I thought I might do better in some of the other exams but I hadn't managed to buy any of the books on those courses either so I'm afraid I was mistaken. In the end sadly I failed everything, particularly music, in which I got O, which was the lowest mark in the history of the college. I parted acrimoniously from the sinister Dr X, who of course passed all his exams with flying colours. Within weeks I was back home in disgrace studying for the repeats and sitting in the café hanging eagerly on every word The Osmonds said. My mother said: 'I'm glad to see you've quit your gallivanting about Cavan,' and I replied: 'Don't worry, Mother – you won't catch me going there again in a hurry!' To which I might have added excitedly: 'And you won't catch me eating acid either!' And she wouldn't either, for happily now those days were long gone, and as I thought of the shade that had once been me, that death-mask of a visage with its chemical-crazed eyes, I took my gold-embossed Keats, once more repairing to my lush pastures and sylvan glades, and as I wandered palely amongst the forlorn heifers and Aberdeen Anguses of 1973, a familiar pang took hold of me and I got to thinking of Threemilehouse Carnival and a slim, pale girl called Marion who 'like ice, like fire', might yet one day be true to me, as a little bird landed on a gate, and somewhere far beyond that grassy Eden, indeed beyond reason itself, a zigzag world as inexplicable as little Jimmy Osmond's chart success, had already begun its inexorable slide towards Saigon, Showaddywaddy, and The Widestripe Suits from Hell.

GRAHAM SWIFT

1974

The balcony in Ano Volos, Greece,
where Graham Swift wrote

NINETEEN SEVENTY-FOUR was the year I failed to write my first novel. It was also the year that the military dictatorship in Greece collapsed almost overnight. The two events are not unconnected. For most of '74 I was living in Greece and it was in Greece, though I didn't know it at the time, that my literary failure occurred.

Having reached the end of my student years – the last three spent posing as a Ph.D. candidate while I secretly began my apprenticeship as a writer – I had answered a dubious advert for teachers with the Strategakis Schools of English, a chain of commercial language schools operating throughout Greece.

It was a fanciful attempt to embrace, or perhaps postpone, my future. It had precedents. There is the fairly well-known case of John Fowles, who went to teach on a magical Greek island and found there the inspiration for a successful novel. I don't recall if I saw myself as following his example. I certainly saw myself under some vine on a veranda conjuring up that – for me unprecedented – thing, a novel.

There was no magical island. I was sent to Volos, an unalluring town on the east coast, largely destroyed by an earthquake in the fifties and gracelessly rebuilt. And the general state of the Strategakis School there can be characterized by the school manager, who met me off the Athens bus, strapped my suitcase to an ancient bicycle and spoke perhaps six words of English.

But I did find a veranda and a vine. It came with the rooms I rented on the edge of town. Thrown in were a little garden and a splendid view. Volos itself may lack glamour but its setting is inspiring. Before me lay the bay from which Jason set forth with the Argonauts. Behind me, cloaked in chestnut woods, rose Mount Pelion, home of the Centaurs.

And one day on my veranda I duly sat down and began to write a novel. There is no point now in disclosing its contents. My memory of it is happily dim. But there I was, fulfilling my vision, intently writing, in the early hours before I went to teach and sometimes late into the night, my first novel.

Voluntary exile is an extraordinarily self-protective thing. Back home there had been the tension between dream and reality. Because I feared the judgement of reality I was my own toughest critic. I tore up perhaps more than I needed to of the stories I wrote. But in Greece I seemed to exist in a state of suspended self-doubt. All questions of appraisal could wait till I returned. The important thing was just to do it.

The vine and the veranda were not always available. The Greek winter is not as mild as Greek summers suggest. More than once I watched the snowline creep down Mount Pelion to engulf me. But winter back home was hardly preferable – this was the crisis winter of Heath's three-day week – and I confess I was not particularly troubled at making my home in a country whose own politics bore no scrutiny at all. Greece in those days was littered with propaganda. In November '73 there were riots, bloodily suppressed, in Athens, and the whole country was plunged under curfew. Six years before, on a previous trip, I had had my own vivid run-in with the Greek authorities when I spent a night in a police station in Thessaloniki after a Greek army officer had accused me (with some reason) of threatening behaviour towards him on a railway station. I was frankly lucky to have suffered no more than a night's detention and a missed train. But I was younger then, and I was not writing a novel.

Winter melted into spring. The air turned ever warmer. A pair of nightingales took up residence in a jasmine bush in my garden. I carried outside the little fold-up table that was all I had for a desk and in the cool of the early hours I would sit with my pen and notepad, listening to the nightingales, breathing jasmine and watching the pink light spread over the hills of Thessaly.

I don't know what happened to the Strategakis School in Volos after my departure in June. Its days were plainly numbered. Its finances and classroom furniture were in ruins. In nine months I had grown attached to its odd mixture of impoverishment, mercenariness and ingenuousness. I was fond of my students, who taught me more Greek than I taught them English, I had made friends in town; and I would miss my veranda.

But the best of my time in Greece was yet to come. I had always intended to stay on when the school year was over and with what was left from my salary to travel at will. I took the bus to Athens, left the bulk of my things with a friend there – including the now quite voluminous, if unfinished manuscript of my novel (it could wait till I was back in England) – and that same evening took the night boat from Piraeus to Lesbos. On the darkening upper deck I met three girls, one English, one American, one Greek, rolling out their sleeping bags. They were going to stay in a little beach house on Lesbos owned by the Greek one's uncle, and asked me if I wanted to come along. I rolled out my sleeping bag next to theirs. Sometimes life is very simple.

In the weeks and months which followed I was as happy, as free, as lucky as I have ever been. I hopped at random around the Aegean and, beginning with that charmed week in Lesbos, idyll followed idyll as island followed island. I went my own way when I wanted to but there was no lack of fellow travellers. I fell in love, certainly in lust, more than once. I knew the country, could speak the language and my saved-up drachmas seemed to last miraculously. I don't recall sparing a thought for literature or making a single note for my novel.

And none of this was greatly altered when in July, following the Turkish invasion of Cyprus and the intensification of the fighting there, all of Greece was mobilized. The life of vagrant hedonism went on, even as guards were mounted and blackouts imposed. I remember sleeping one night on a beach on Kos – just across the water from the Turkish mainland – and being woken by the rumble of trucks and the shouts of orders as an army convoy moved along the island's perimeter road. In the troop-carriers were young conscripts of my age. I turned over and looked back up at the stars.

But before the summer was out even Greeks had cause for joy. In the wake of the threat of full-scale war, which never materialized, the seven-year-old junta dissolved – a military tyranny brought down by military exigency. The realization that this had indeed happened spread, even in the remote Aegean, like some quickening breeze. I had never seen a whole people touched by political glee before. I should perhaps have reflected that while Greeks had still been oppressed I had been having the time of my life – what right had I to share in this new happiness? What I think I felt was that events had only crowned my own lease of bliss. It was time to go home. I would leave the country on a high note.

Some while after my return to England I got out the manuscript of my novel, began to read it and knew at once that it was awful. Irredeemably awful. Strangely, this lucid realization didn't devastate me. I have abandoned work since with greater agony. I didn't feel that those days on the veranda had been wasted or that those weeks in the Aegean sun were a delusion. No, the judgement I could now pass on myself would have poisoned those days. Those days were inviolate. Let life be lived.

None the less, what I had written was crap.

The future had caught up with me but I would not let it trap me. I found sporadic work as a part-time teacher – teaching again – in various south London colleges. I have never had any vocation or training as a teacher but for the next ten years this was how I survived. The part-time status was as vital to my self-esteem – I would never be sucked into full-time employ-ment – as it was in giving me time each day to write. And during those ten years, without the aid of a single vine leaf or veranda, I did indeed write, and publish, not only my first novel but two others.

I remember standing one morning that autumn in a crowded suburban railway station on my way to one of my colleges. Barely a month before I had been dallying in the Dodecanese. Few sights are less exalting, more chilling to the soul than the sight of English commuters massing for the daily grind, and there was I – who had once on another railway platform jeered at a strutting Greek army officer – clutching my briefcase. But I had the oddly uplifting sensation of being at a turning-point.

After that winter of oil crisis and three-day weeks there were two general elections. In America Nixon resigned. The aura, the taste of a decade lingers over into the next and I can't help feeling that the spirit of the sixties, that surge of post-war optimism and liberalism in which I was lucky enough to have been young, really died in 1974. Perhaps for me it was artificially extended, its edges blurred, by my time in Greece. I had entered my mid-twenties. When does youth end?

But if the chill was entering my soul on that railway platform it was partly because I had no inkling that wonderful things were still in store for me in that benign year, and they were to happen not in Calymnos or Kos but in Clapham . . .

There cannot be many moments in your life when you appreciate you are at a watershed. The autumn of '74 was one. It was the year in which I more than once knew perfect happiness. It was the year in which I became aware, in more than one way, of historical forces. And it was the year in which, contrary to the evidence, I knew I would be a writer.

RUSSELL HOBAN

1975

A drawing of Punch made by Russell Hoban
while he was working on Riddley Walker

T HE LINE BETWEEN time and space is always blurred: people say, 'after Munich' or 'after Dallas' when they want to place in time a complex of event, atmosphere, mood, and political conditions. 'We'll always have Paris,' says Ingrid Bergman to Humphrey Bogart in *Casablanca*. Every history is a palimpsest of geographies, whether great or tiny; even a recluse who rarely goes out traces the geography of his days from one room to another between the yellowing years stratified in old newspapers stacked in the hall.

Amazing, how the past doesn't go away. Facing myself in the morning mirror I see the sun through the leaves over roads I'll never drive again, smell the wood-smoke of old autumns, hear the rasp of crows on the winds of departed springs, the whisper of rain and the hiss of tyres on streets long gone. And songs! A chaos, a confusion, an utter tohu bohu of songs from which words and tunes rise up inexplicably:

I took a trip on a train and I thought about you.

Understandable. But

> *It's a big holiday everywhere, for the Jones family has a brand-new heir.*
> *He's a joy heaven-sent, and we proudly present*
> *Mr Franklin D. Roosevelt Jones!*

Where's that coming from and why?

You better get Wildroot Cream Oil, Charlie, to keep your hair in trim!

Please, enough!

Places. How is it that some places were alive in me before I ever saw them? The Judaean desert unrolling mile after mile the dry scrolls of its time and the boat-shaped rock of Masada clamorous with silent voices; the Caspar David Friedrich sunset over the River Aller in the Lower Saxony town of Celle and the flatlands receding in the dusk to Bergen-Belsen and beyond. Yes, I thought, walking by that river with my Celle-born wife, I recognize this very European and not at all American river. My dead parents (the dead, being of the past, never go away) also know this river, not specifically as the Aller but as any dark and sunset river in the Ukraine where they were born. A river shining under the darkening sky and in the dimness the level miles going away to other times – yes, that river is in me and of me, and when in 1975 I married this woman who grew up by the Aller there took place in us a great mingling and amalgamation of geographies, all the times and places lived and inherited by the two of us combining orchestrally their themes and motifs and the coloration of their many voices.

We met in London in 1970. She was employed by Truslove & Hanson in Sloane Street as a book siren; I used to go into the shop looking for one book and come out with seven or eight. In the countries where we were born each of us had felt a stranger so we were both comfortable here where we actually were strangers. Our marriage, following as it did a divorce, divided my life in two and made permanent my strangerhood in Europe; it acknowledged formally all manner of recognitions and resonances. How is it that the unknown is always familiar? When I find myself on a dark road late at night in the middle of nowhere in a pouring rain it seems quite natural. I think that's because strangeness is the esential human condition. My body forgets pain and my mind forgets joy but the strangeness is there always.

Life is continuous; in my memory it doesn't separate itself neatly into numbered years because each year contains all those before it. Trying to recall the taste of London in my eyes in 1975 I see a red telephone box in the rain under the drooping white blossoms of a chestnut tree. Just that at first, fresh and juicy in the memory – the red telephone box in the rain and the white petals scattered on it. As a telephone box it has no significance beyond its ordinary function; I never made or received an important call there. But it stands near the block of flats where we lived for the first two years we were together, the book siren and I. Colour is more so at some times than at others, and the remembered red of that telephone box is for me the concentrated visible essence of a time in my life when I had what I wanted when I wanted it.

With the telephone box come the wet bronze of the

female nude on the Embankment near the Albert Bridge, the lights on the bridge against a sky still light on a spring evening, the high-tide Thames lapping against the water steps, the low-tide Thames narrow between its mud beaches. When I went jogging in the mornings my mind sang over and over two lines from Schiller's *Sayings of Confucius* to the tune of a Haydn symphony the number of which I've forgotten:

> *Nur die Fülle führt zur Klarheit,*
> *Und im Abgrund wohnt die Wahrheit.*

> Only fullness leads to clarity,
> And truth dwells in the abyss.

The images of the telephone box, the chestnut tree, the bronze nude, the Albert Bridge, the Thames and its tides – they're actually from when we lived in Beaufort Street; we moved to Fulham in 1972 but those mind-pictures are part of the geographical union that was legalized in 1975.

The city – any city – is a construct of the collective mind, a labyrinth of mirrors, some bright, some dark. The city is an arrangement of boxes and passageways and ups and downs thought into place. In the country the boxes and mirrors of the self are in a different conjunction of time and space. In 1975 I was often in Kent for *Riddley Walker* research. I remember a place not far from the town of Wye: we drove up a very steep dirt track and stopped on the high ground overlooking a little valley and the house, sheds, and outbuildings of a snug farm. Crows were soaring below us and the air seemed alive with the long-ago vibrations from prey to hunter that the roaming raider must have felt looking down from where we stood. Maybe there never was a raider looking down from that spot – that doesn't matter; in that place there lives the recurrent quantum wave of what might have happened. That overlook, like the telephone box, signifies a time in my life, the strangeness of the five and a half years when I was working on that novel.

I open my 1975 diary to today's date, December 14th, and I find: *Riddley Walker on 411*. By the time I finished it on Guy Fawkes Day, 1979, it was down to 220 pages. The beginning of it was on March 14th, 1974, when I saw Canterbury Cathedral for the first time. The look of the soaring fan vaulting was like that great burst of sound in Haydn's *Die Schöpfung*: '*und es ward Licht!*' I remember the vaulting as being so full of lift that the columns, rather than supporting it, seemed to be tethering it to the floor. And above the echoing murmurs and footsteps I felt all around me in the layered fullness of the air the silent hum of centuries.

Walking slowly, I saw many things of which I remember only the Pilgrims' Steps and the place where Thomas Becket was murdered. After a time I found myself in the North Aisle standing before a faint tracery of earth-green lines on a white wall, all that remained of the fifteenth-century wall painting, *The Legend of Saint*

Eustace. On the other side of the aisle, in sections, was the reconstruction by E. W. Tristram with a text describing the episodes leading to Eustace's martyrdom.

The story begins with Eustace hunting. He sees 'a stag, between whose antlers appears the figure of the crucified Saviour'. Eustace embarks on a pilgrimage with his wife and two little sons. His wife is taken off by pirates. Eustace and his sons reach a river. He swims across with one boy, then returns for the other. When in the middle of the river he sees a wolf carrying off the first child and a lion the second. 'We see St Eustace praying in the midst of the river,' says the text. I looked at Eustace treading water and hoping for better times and I knew how it was with him. That was where *Riddley Walker* began.

Something else came into that beginning. There are certain ideas that I consider elemental: Orpheus and Eurydice, Miranda and Caliban, Fay Wray and King Kong are among them. There are endless variants of these stories of love and loss, of rage and desire and death; the ideas are always cruising around looking for people who will keep them going in one form and another. Punch and Judy are of this class of idea. 'Punch is so old he can't die,' the great puppeteer Percy Press once told me. 'He's a law unto himself.' This ancient anarch lurking in the dark corridors of my brain jumped into the front of my mind while I was looking at Eustace treading water and there came to me the post-apocalyptic Inland of Riddley Walker, a desolate England regressed to a mostly Iron Age culture, the inhabitants living in fenced-in settlements while packs of killer dogs roam the land and such government as there is makes its policies known through shows performed by itinerant puppeteers.

Never before and never since have I been lucky enough to have so much come to me for the start of a novel. But my workroom is littered with unfinished starts and I dared not take anything for granted in 1974. There are two reasons for choosing 1975 to write about; one was that by then the thing had taken me firmly in its jaws and didn't look like letting go: Riddley Walker, digging for old iron at Widders Dump, had come up with a blackened Punch figure and was over the fence, off with the dogs, and into his story. In 1975 Riddley's journey permanently established a particular kind of connection between this place and me. The other reason for my choice of year is that as some doors closed, others opened, and the book siren and I legalized the putting together of our two geographies as one history. A memorable year.

IAN McEWAN

1976

US Notebook

Ian McEwan on his travels in the United States

In 1976, at the age of twenty-seven, I visited the United States for the first time.

26 April, New York

The real price of my cheap flight from Amsterdam is to arrive in New York at 4.00 a.m. Steven Gerber kindly meets me in his mother's car. As we drive towards Rego Park my first impressions have a lambent stupidity: so they have *cats* in America, and lampposts, and children's playgrounds, and trees with the same bright spring greenery. The USA confessing to human touches nicely at odds with the sheen of my fantasies.

Later in the morning, while Steven visits his psychoanalyst, I go off in search of my old friend, John Milich. An eleven-dollar cab ride down Ocean Avenue which runs in a straight line to the ends of the earth. The apartment building is dark and smelly. I knock on a couple of doors. Chunky locks and door chains. A suspicious woman speaks through the chink. No one's ever heard of John. I wish I hadn't had my hair cut. I feel pink and jug-eared and hesitant.

I wait for a bus to take me back into town. A lady in the queue gives me directions and a handy lesson on the avenue/street arrangement in Manhattan. I tell her

41

I'll be going to Maine. In that case, she says, you gotta visit Quebec. Oh, I say, too laconically, I'll see what my host has in store. She comes back quick: I hope he's kind enough to allow ya a little freedom.

The arrangement is that I'll meet Steven at Columbia University, but on the bus going uptown I fall into a daydream and get off two or three blocks late. The bus roars away and I'm standing on an abandoned mattress. Virtually no traffic, no white faces and very quiet. I start walking. A group of kids on a corner call out to me, Hey you! but they don't bother to cross the street to where I am. I walk briskly, as though I have some business here. The street is getting worse – lots of places boarded up, and every inch of pavement looks fought over. Squalor and boredom. Where are all those yellow taxis? My mouth is dry and the sweat is itching down my back. This is what I was warned against. With my short hair and leather case I look like a government official, a rent collector. I've been here less than twelve hours and I'm going to be mugged. I'll be one of those cautionary tales that give such pleasure. A man comes towards me wearing a suit and tie. When I ask for directions he looks at me wonderingly. But he is friendly. The route he gives is complicated. At all costs I must avoid the small wedge of park I have glimpsed down side streets. If you walk that way, he says reasonably, you're going to get *taken off*, because you're a white man. He gives more directions but I am no longer concentrating. When he has gone, I walk on and head for the sound of traffic. Every loud voice gives me a jolt. It's a matter of minutes before I am taken off. I attach myself to a group of women with shopping bags. My stupid grin is to indicate that I am a part of their happy conversation. We round a corner. Two hundred yards ahead I see an intersection with traffic whizzing through. I run towards it and hail a cab.

28 April, New York

After two days honing my Harlem story, I realize that everyone has something similar to tell. The impulse to make it humorous: at the time you are in the garden of forking paths. Down here, death, or a lifetime in a wheelchair, or a cracked skull and permanent mental damage, or at the very least, street paranoia for ever cemented into your life skills; down another path, a funny story at dinner. Choose.

I go to meet Philip Roth in his apartment. I tell my Harlem tale. He offers a scare story of his own. These are ritual preliminaries. We embark on a long conversation oddly compounded of intimacy and abstraction. He says he feels he no longer knows anything about the world, that his work is at a crisis because *My Life as a Man* was the end of a line of development. I tell him how difficult I'm finding it, writing a novel. Perhaps I'll never write one. He says, Of course you will. You don't have any choice. His manner is quizzical, teasing,

43

vaguely avuncular. Gentle, courteous, but with a manic gleam, a taste for mayhem. We talk about sex. The cycle of relationships, passion disintegrating into friendship. How to make love and work fit. I tell him I'm in love. He asks if it interferes with writing. I say, of course. We talk about the fear of loneliness; he admits that the solitude he wrote of with relish in *Reading Myself* omitted to mention the woman he was living with. Then, the inanity of critics – he has given up explaining himself, and no longer has any idea why he writes and who he writes for. The only *tangible* return is the money he earns. He is a rich man . . . but he knows nothing. He talked himself out of one affair because he couldn't commit to having children. I say that I too cannot imagine being a father. He says he can easily imagine me as one. I ask him to disentangle for me the fact and the fiction in *My life as a Man*. The marriage was truly terrible, he says. Some of the best parts, though (the poker, when she shits herself) turn out to be inventions.

He constantly shifts his position in his chair. He has a pain up his arms and across his neck. It hurts less when he walks, so we set off to a Hungarian restaurant. I praise, 'I only wanted you to admire my fasting.' We talk about Kafka's loneliness, how he found love only when he was dying in Berlin, away from his father's city. It's very easy to like Philip Roth. The intelligence is warm, with a touch of cruelty to keep you alert. Easy to imagine women falling in love with him. His pillow talk is probably an enchantment – funny, obscene, fond. He pays for the lunch and walks me to the subway station.

2 May, New York

I am sharing a tiny room with Steven in his parents' apartment in Rego Park. Our beds are barely three feet apart. Steven takes me to a fish restaurant on Long Island. In the night I wake knowing that I am about to throw up. Before I have even put one leg on the floor it happens – with such force it seems to propel me backwards. Way of getting to the moon? Fortunately, it is Sunday. The floor is strewn with the several dozen sections of *The New York Times*. Steven is very decent and unsqueamish about it.

Fifth Avenue. Self-importantly, I enter a sky-scraper, on legitimate business like everyone else. I visit – in his office. Towards the end of our chat he produces from his desk a jiffy bag of Colombian grass. To see me on my travels. In the evening we visit a friend of Steven's, a sweet, hospitable cultivated gay who lives in a penthouse on Riverside Drive. A long talk about Corso and Ginsberg. When I produce the grass, our host brings out a pipe in the form of an engorged cock and balls made of fleshy pink ceramic. You put the grass

45

in an indentation in the balls, and suck on the cock. Not wishing to appear homophobic, we apply ourselves manfully.

5 May, To Waterville, Maine

On the train. The easy brevity of two American strangers. No modifiers. Where'd'ya find the beer? Two cars back! In England you'd get: Excuse me. Sorry to trouble you, but I couldn't help noticing the beer can in your hand. Would you mind awfully pointing me in the direction of the . . .

27 May, Buffalo

After a week's heel-kicking I have a year-old white Toyota Celica to deliver to the docks in San Francisco inside eight days. I have to hunt for an hour through the nightmare ruins of Buffalo to find Route 90. And then the whole continent stretches ahead. The temperature is 80°F, the sky yellow-white with urban poison, the land on this southern stretch of Lake Eerie is flat and despoiled, the traffic, four or five lanes of cars and trucks moving within a narrow speed band, the car radio is AM only, and a good song is hard to find. But my heart soars. I whoop and holler over the roar of the wind. The joy of motion-at-last, of so much land ahead, of a journey like those in the days of horses, a journey of days and nights.

2 June, Harben, Utah

I pick up hitch-hikers everywhere. The first, outside Buffalo, is a desperado in a leather jacket carrying a bedroll. He gets in without saying hello. We smoke a companionable joint and he still doesn't want to talk. I lapse happily into my own thoughts. When I set my passenger down he gets out without saying goodbye. Oddly satisfying.

I pick up Catherine from Philadelphia. Now she lives in Tucson, Arizona, and wants to be a cowgirl. She wears a stetson and even chews tobacco. She puts her boots up on the dashboard – not easy in a Toyota. We stop off in Dinosaur, Utah, and go out along a cat walk to observe a man chipping away at the vertical face of what was once a river bed. A whole dinosaur is emerging. Catherine scrunches up her face and asks me to explain. It turns out she is extremely short-sighted. Why don't you get glasses? She says, I don't like sharp details. I'm into diffusion. I leave her at her camp under a clump of cottonwoods, surrounded by limestone outcrops weathered into strange shapes – real cowgirl country but invisible to her – and set off in the evening towards Salt Lake City. The road drops downhill for so many miles that I fantasize that I'm descending into

Hades. But it levels out in Harben, another neon strip. I phone John Webb in Vancouver from a public booth. When I'm finished and getting back in the car, the phone rings. I know it's the operator wanting me to pay for extra time. From the car I look at the starkly lit booth, and the phone ringing – for me! A strange dread takes hold of me. And later that night, down a remote country track, I see the first headlights for almost an hour in the rear mirror and the dark impossibility comes down – I'm being followed. Men with guns, some hard American craziness. I can't argue it away. I drive faster. The fear is on me. I've come seven hundred miles in a day. Time to stop.

3 June

. . . I leave Salt Lake City after lunch. A swim in the lake on the way out. Very itchy. Then I go barrelling out across the salt flats, down an infinite avenue of telegraph poles, an empty straight road that disappears into a shimmering heat mirror. Barely visible mountains in the distance. I stop and set out across the desert. Reflected heat blasts up in my face. The surface is composed of crystals of salt formed into little waves. Nothing moves except the heat-warped air. Nothing can grow. Imagine nineteenth-century immigrants crossing this in wagons to the Californian nirvana . . .

At a truck stop I take on board John. His 'lifeplan'

he says is to become a beautician, but for now he's settled for running dope for his uncle. Stopping late at night, there is only one room in the motel, so we share. He keeps me awake with snores and a vile munching noise.

13 June, Pebble Beach, Carmel

The house is shaped like an opened oyster shell, facing out towards the Pacific. The estate is ringed by security fences and patrolled by armed guards and dogs. Our hosts are well-to-do Irish Americans. They have some neighbours in and barbecue giant slabs of prime beef. We get serious with the wine. The IRA is extolled and a toast proposed. I demur, but that is to be expected because I am the English oppressor. We have to do turns. Mine is to read from the op-ed pages in an English voice. A woman sings 'My Funny Valentine', holding Maggie's eyes all the while. One of the husbands, who has a degenerative brain condition and doesn't know who or where he is, wanders off into the night and is brought back by the security guards. I am established early in the evening, on the basis of my remaindered volume of stories, as an author. A copy is handed round. The lady with the demented husband retires across the room to read it. She soon snaps it shut and doesn't speak to me again, even when it's time to say goodbye . . .

15 June, Berkeley

I meet Seamus Heaney who invites me to his poetry class. This is his last at Berkeley. Towards the end he gives a little speech in a soft, fatherly voice, telling the students how much he has enjoyed teaching them. Then the kids produce their gifts – mostly handmade. A huge cardigan, carved wooden toys for his children, a painting, an illustrated poem, an old silver dollar, something in clay. People are sighing and shaking their heads. One girl puts her face in her hands and cries. The poet is taking his wisdom and kindness away across the sea. Soon everyone is tearful. Seamus, please don't go!

30 June, British Columbia

Five hours to the east of Vancouver . . . is the Mediter-ranean. Sage and thyme, olive trees, oranges and lemons sold at the road side. We are sleeping under the shooting stars in a cherry orchard on the banks of Lake Okanagan which winds through the mountains like a wide river. Susan Brown's house is beautifully ramshackle. There's an old jetty, a sauna in the boat house. The paradise days have begun. We eat *Psilocybe* mushrooms, canoe, swim naked in the electric-cold water, take saunas, play volley ball, drink wine and talk about Jimmy Carter, and Ezra Pound, on whom Tom is an authority . . . two days later we are sleeping out on the remote southern edge of Lake Chilliwack backed by a rainforest of gigantic ferns and loopy purple flowers. Surely one of the most blessed parts of the earth . . . we plan our journey in Stan's big Chevy – eastward to the Rockies, then a great arc through badlands and desert to LA . . . and so it begins . . . in lush meadows along the Belly River, across from the Blood Indian reservation . . . we make the long walk through the woods into the USA, then back, an almost full moon, the yellow grasses along the river shining white . . . and cook steaks on our fire . . . and onwards, to the alpine meadows of Glacier Park where we stroll in seas of Indian paintbrush plants . . . onwards to Flathead Lake where we swim out towards the setting sun . . . and down through plains of golden grass to cowboy town Missoula to clean up after five nights under the sky, and play pool . . . and on at last to the Bitterroot River and its beautiful banks of sand . . . no houses for sixty miles, until North Fork where John lands two fat steelhead trout to roast over our fire . . . the pace and exhilaration of the trip gathers, now we are in a dream, consumed by the Journey . . . onwards to the high meadows of Morgan mountain where it is still spring, where great spreads of nameless flowers in oranges, reds, and blues are banked along the north fork of the Salmon River, where Lewis and Clarke first made their trail in 1805 and where a washed-out gold mine sits across from where we camp . . . southwards along the Salmon River, swimming every hour, watching the rich forests give way to sagebrush desert . . . and camp in a meadow by July 4th Creek and climb a bluff to see the Sawtooth Mountains . . . (have I ever been, will I ever be happier? Simply my body, without thoughts. Joyous intoxication. I am blessed by fortune, friends, vitality, dazzled by open spaces, I could travel for ever across this country. Could I bear to sleep indoors every night? Or be back inside myself? I never want to write another thing, and I don't want England, London, Stockwell. Only Penny. Two weeks to go) . . . now westward across the desert, in and out of the tangle of San Francisco in four days, and south again, (*22 July*) to camp where the Big Sur River runs into the ocean . . . at midday, 150 micrograms of LSD . . . we follow a trail which takes us higher and higher through fields of golden wild corn. The ocean drops below us, inland the sinuous yellow hills with lines of trees marking the water courses . . . we enter groves of redwoods . . . like stepping into a cathedral . . . all afternoon the trail unwinds before us, dipping and rolling round the hills . . . in an amphitheatre of flowers, a small yellow pond drying in the heat, steam rising off it like a soup, and it *is* – a life soup, for the mud is moving, seething with a million baby frogs crawling in the deep cracks . . . we wonder about poetry and landscape – the final geography of consciousness, landscape the correlative for the soul in transcendence, and we quote scraps of Wallace Stevens' *The Credences of Summer* . . . the sun is dropping into the ocean as we turn and jog back bare-chested, effortlessly for miles across high pastures and down into the lush river valley . . . it is dark when we reach the inn. Without a thought, we step out of our clothes into the heated outdoor pool, call over the waiter, go drifting up and down in the steam with our bourbons . . . can these pleasures keep coming? The manager, magically backlit, looms and in sepulchral voice, like one who brings to an end the revels and madness of a Shakespeare comedy, orders our innocent naked selves out of his pool. It ain't right, he says, and I know it ain't right . . . and he's right, his words are the bells that toll us back from the infinite to the world of reasonable and common observances. Four days to go, my airline ticket says. We get dressed in the chilly night air, grinning like Fools . . .

CHARLES NICHOLL

1977

Sally and William

I T W A S T H E year of the Jubilee, and the year of Punk, and so for me a year of not really belonging, identifying neither with the patriotism of the great royal tea-party, nor with the rant of the Sex Pistols singing 'God Save The Queen'. I was one of those whom the punks outmoded. Youth was wearing safety pins and pink Mohicans, and I was not. Suddenly, at the age of twenty-six, I wasn't young any more.

It was going to be a year of change: I knew that from the start. When the year began, I was broke and broadly speaking jobless and my girlfriend was pregnant. The first two situations were familiar enough – work and money were fluid commodities, sometimes one had both and sometimes one had neither – but the third was entirely new to me.

Sally was four months gone. It was past the time of concealment: it had been announced. We called the baby 'he' – correctly, as it turned out – and knowing that he still might choose not to be, we nicknamed him Hamlet.

We felt good about it, rather heroic, brought close together by the adventure of it. It was like setting off on a journey: something we were going to do alone. Her pregnancy was already absenting us from that easy communal life we had drifted in for years.

★

There is a picture of Sally, black-haired and round-bellied, wearing a mauve dress, standing against that dark grey London brick which is itself somewhat mauve in certain lights. This must be January: there is winter jasmine on the wall, and by February we had left London and moved to the country.

At the time this seemed a bold move. It was only later that we realized how conformist it was: all over London there were middle-class couples in their late twenties, visibly swelling with first children and thoughts of change, piling cartons of LPs into clapped-out old cars, and heading off for The Country. We didn't know them then, but we have met them since. Some of them are our friends and neighbours in this rural ghetto where we have come to rest.

So it turns out we were merely part of a sociological phenomenon, a small diaspora. Or perhaps we were just obeying our instincts, and setting about a rather complex form of 'nesting'. Either way, it's odd how the clutter and particularity of one's life proves, in retrospect, to be part of a pattern; to be impelled by things one did not see at the time.

By the end of February we were settled in our new home on the edge of a Somerset village. This was not at all the thatched tea-cosy world of a *Country Living* spread. We were house-sitting for a friend who had gone to India. We lived in what the estate agents would call the 'granny flat'. It was new, and built above the garage. It looked out over long fields that exuded at dusk an icy grey air which licked up through the floorboards, through the cut-price carpeting, through the warped windows.

In the ice and mud of those first weeks we suspected we had made a dreadful mistake – not realizing that every subsequent February spent in the English countryside would also feel like a dreadful mistake – but then the spring came, and the fields erupted with buttercups, and the grey woods glittered, and the air of the lanes dizzied us with the dust of cow-parsley, and we knew that after all we were right to be here.

There was an elegiac note, for this was also the year of Dutch elm disease: the landscape was scarred with dead trees, a Gothic vision of pale skeleton hands clawing up from a graveyard. But in that first spring we felt those things which have kept us in the country ever since: to be in touch with the elements; to be intimate with the seasons; to look in on the secrecy of wild places; to be independent, solitary, self-regulating, sceptical; to live – a quaint phrase I always like – unto yourself.

There is much about life in a country village that is narrow and snobbish, suburban in all but location, but everywhere we have lived we have found at least one kindly, philosophical countryman, a torchbearer of almost vanished country rhythms and values. Let me now praise John Pike, Tom Smith, Jack Jones, Tom

Lloyd and all the others: handymen, farmworkers, gardeners; leaners on the spade-handle of life.

Tom Lloyd would see me flailing incompetently at our overgrown lawn with an old machete, and a few minutes later he'd be down there proffering his scythe – 'Here, he'll fetch it off for you.' Tom performed many different jobs with great expertise, but they mostly came down to some form of 'fetching'. Grass was fetched off by his scythe, soot was fetched down by his chimney-brush, blockages were fetched through by his drain-rods, and on one occasion, after I had over-indulged in the local pub, our car was fetched up from a ditch by his tractor.

Sally gave birth to our son – or 'fetched him out', as Tom would have said – on an afternoon in May, after an arduous thirty-hour labour.

She can doubtless remember the labour better than I do, as she was the one who was labouring. I have only a sense of an immensely long period of disjointed activity. Sometimes I was sleeping in an armchair; sometimes I was doing the crossword, and jotting down the times of her contractions in the margin; and sometimes I was clasping her hand during the terrible punctuations of pain and effort. These were still the early days of fathers in the delivery room: the role was even less clear than it is now.

Then came a sudden moment of crisis, the donning of the Dr Kildare face-mask, and Sally in the last throes, which seemed strangely sexual, a sense that this pain was a mirror of the pleasures which had put this creature inside her in the first place.

And then, slithering out with a sudden and quite unexpected aplomb, he was there. We have had other babies since, and they have been the traditional kind, raspberry-coloured and understandably disgruntled, but William came into the world with a serene, pallid, already child-like face.

Thus we discovered the mystery, the simple arithmetic truth we had been preparing for and which the first child reveals most powerfully: that a moment ago there were two of us, and now there were three.

After it was all over, and mother and baby were sleeping, I strolled out into the sunshine, and ate a hearty meal, and then dropped in to watch the closing stages of the county cricket match. I was rewarded with the sight of Vivian Richards in full flow. He came in with a few overs to go, and by stumps he had scored 48 not out, all in fours. It seemed everything that I could wish for my son in his life to come: power and grace, effortless poise, and a pleasant undertone of the exotic: a touch of black magic in the agreeable shadow of Bath Abbey on an evening in May.

★

Not long after this we decided to get married. When we phoned up a friend and told her we needed a witness, she said, 'Oh God, have you had an accident?'

The wedding took place on Midsummer Day at Bath Registry Office. It was a rather furtive, slapdash affair, with our infant in tow. It was nearly called off at the last minute, as the registrar insisted on cash, and of course we had none. Our one and only wedding photograph has an eerie quality, as something was wrong with the camera, and we are shadowed in our nuptial moment by two pale ghosts, though whether from the past or the future I do not know. I am wearing an ageing Take 6 suit, and Sally is in Afghan jewellery and a flower-print dress, both of us haggard from the first weeks of parenthood.

We were going to have a wedding tea in the Pump Rooms, but they were closed, and we had tea in the cafeteria instead. William cried, the car broke down on Lansdowne Hill on the way back, our witnesses had to get home, and we sat watching TV, which seemed that night to show nothing but sit-coms predicated on the doleful trials and tribulations – the deep intrinsic tiredness – of married couples.

We took the point: marriages survive on laughter, at least as much as on love, and sometimes more so.

The following day I received the news that my first book had found a publisher, and so in the space of a few weeks I became a father, a husband and an author. I do not have much sense that I *made* these things happen. One exercises care and choice in the little things, but in the important matters life gives you what you have, and some day takes it away again.

This was a year of letting go, of stepping off the carousel and finding ourselves on solid earth, our pockets empty and our arms laden with riches.

CARYL PHILLIPS

1978

Caryl Phillips' NUS card for 1978-9

THE YEAR is 1978. The place, Oxford. The month, October. The photograph might have been taken in a photo-booth at Gloucester Green Bus Station. Or in one somewhere behind Broad Street. Or in one just off Cornmarket. I simply can't remember. I must have recently had my hair cut, for in 1978 I used to wear it long. Or, more accurately, wide. In those days even Michael Jackson had an afro. Not that I wanted to be Michael Jackson. Not then. Not now. In 1978 my people were Earth, Wind and Fire. Wide hair, funky clothes, thumping, danceable rhythms. 'Boogie Wonderland', 'Got To Get You Into My Life', 'September'. In 1978 they 'conquered' Britain. As did *Saturday Night Fever*. Both the movie and the album. Oxford was full of over-confident young men in white suits, pumping their pelvises in time to 'Night Fever'. Disco was having a last, desperate throw of the dice. Punk had muscled in on the scene. For those of us who took unashamed pleasure in sporting flares and platform soles, things were heading rapidly downhill. In 1978 a man named Jilted John tortured us with a spectacularly inept single entitled 'Gordon Is A Moron'. Ian Dury and the Blockheads livened things up a little by hitting us with their rhythm sticks, but, all things considered, 1978 marked the end of an era for the generation who had come in with Gary Glitter, Marc Bolan and Ziggy Stardust. In

October 1978 I had my photograph taken for my National Union of Students card. I was embarking upon my third and final year as a student. Decisions would have to be made. Freedom lay just around the corner, as of course did the ominous presence of Mrs Thatcher.

At the start of 1978 I still clung to the idea of being a theatre director. In March of that year I directed what turned out to be my last production: Ibsen's *Ghosts*. The redeeming feature of this production was a startling performance by a brilliant actor in the role of Oswald. I haven't seen Adam Thorpe for some years, but he now lives in France with his wife and children, and writes both poetry and prose. We toured the production all over England, to what the critics call 'mixed reviews'. After our last night, in Durham as it turned out, I wheeled Adam around the ancient streets in a hastily borrowed wheelbarrow. He played his saxophone. I whooped and hollered appreciatively. We were both alcoholically challenged. We parked by the moonlit River Wear and Adam continued to play. Then a fish leapt clear – a salmon? – I've no idea. I swear it did a triple toe-loop. I gave it 9 for degree of difficulty, and 9.5 for artistic impression. We stared blankly at each other. Then I wheeled him back to our lodgings. The following morning I woke up to find a police officer staring down at me. 'OK, son, where's your Joe Loss friend?' It appeared that one of Adam's more sinewy solos had been delivered beneath the window of the Vice-

Chancellor of Durham University. Adam and I 'beat the rap', but I never directed again. And he never acted.

In the summer of 1978 I made two decisions which subsequently changed the course of my life. I decided to go to the United States, courtesy of Freddie Laker's Skytrain. This would mark the first time that I would leave Britain since arriving as a screaming infant from the Caribbean in the late fifties. This would also be my first time in an aeroplane. In short, I decided to undertake the biggest adventure of my life. For five weeks I travelled aimlessly on Greyhound buses, reading, thinking, watching, dreaming. I travelled from New York to Los Angeles. From Detroit to San Francisco. I went to Canada. To Mexico. I 'discovered' Baldwin, Wright, Ellison, George Jackson, Malcolm X. For the first time in my life I had time to think about England objectively, to think about the Caribbean, to think about myself. And, funnily enough, no longer did it seem appealing that I should spend the rest of my life locked up in rehearsal rooms with Ibsen, Tennessee Williams, Shakespeare et al. The United States removed the blinkers from my eyes, and made me aware that the accident of my birth had perhaps prepared me for something other than directing plays. In the United States I encountered an unapologetic, upwardly mobile black middle-class. A group of people who dared to aspire, who, quite rightly, did not regard themselves as immigrants, and who were therefore not subject to the nervous hesitancy which characterizes the lives of new arrivants, whether black or white. In the United States I discovered, by reading and observing, that I had a common history with black Americans, and I wanted to write about them. And about myself. I wasn't really sure what I wanted to say, or if indeed I had anything to say, but I *knew* – with alarming conviction – that I wanted to write. I now realized that I belonged to a larger tradition than that of black working-class kids from Yorkshire, who spoke like Freddie Trueman. I returned to Oxford in October 1978 a very different person from the one who had left five weeks earlier.

The photograph might have been taken in a photo-booth at Gloucester Green Bus Station. Or in one somewhere behind Broad Street. Or in one just off Cornmarket. I simply can't remember. However, what I do remember is feeling that I had only one more year to survive. Yes, survive. Before I embarked upon the adventure of being a writer. I looked into the camera and made a mischievous gesture of defiance. But beneath the irony, my mind was set. 'Home' from America. One more year to go. I used to take great delight in watching people's faces whenever I presented my union card. But my mind *was* set. I had changed. I threw away my flares and platform soles. For the first time I could see beyond Oxford. The Irish writer Brian Moore said recently that the door closes on a writer at twenty. This may well be the case. If so then my door closed with this photograph. In 1978. And another door opened.

JIM CRACE

1979

Hearts of Oak

Jim Crace held by his father

I SEEMED TO spend the whole year in the air. I had been complaining to the commissioning editors of the *Sunday Telegraph Magazine* – with whom I had a freelance 'retainer' – that I was tired of home-based journalism. I wanted up; I wanted out; I wanted foreign travel. The pestering paid off. I flew to Montserrat in the Leewards to interview George Martin at his new recording studios, to New York to meet – or fail to meet, as it turned out – the singer Debbie Harry of Blondie, to California to drive Pacific Highway One for a travel piece, to the metal fortresses of Piper and Forties to report on disaster control in the North Sea oilfields. I found myself – on the magazine's behalf – 'rescued from drowning' off the Lizard in Cornwall by a Wessex 5 helicopter. The unnamed 'High Wire Hero' in the four-page colour spread swinging from a 300-foot winch-line above a stroppy sea was me, courageous for a fee, reckless on expenses.

But most of the spring of 1979 – that spring which closed so cheerlessly on May 3rd with Thatcher, newly elected on the steps of Number Ten, predicting 'harmony and hope' – was taken up by two long-winded journalistic tasks. One was a report on Britain's 'top surgeons'; the other involved more flights than I had pestered for. I was asked to investigate and test for the magazine the variable passenger services of Britain's 'third level' commuter airlines, the modest independent short-haul island-hoppers, the cost-cutters, the shove-'em-in-and-slam-the-door sky's-the-limit fly-by-nights, all with flights as divorced from intercontinental jet travel as a bike is from a Bentley. I sped between airfields and operating theatres like some self-locating donor organ. At Derbyshire Royal Infirmary, neuro-surgeon and aerobatics pilot John Firth kitted me out in sterile cap, gown, mask and wellies and ushered me into an operating theatre to inspect 'the plumbing' of a gaping cranium. 'Don't admit you're a journalist,' he said. 'If anybody asks, say you're an aerobatics friend.' Someone did ask, of course. I extemporized the pleasure of doing loops and dives in my Pitts Special. I'd been airborne enough that spring to play the pilot with careless ease.

It was not a time that I was glad to be so close to surgeons. Charley Crace, my dad, had learned that the relentless ulcer which had plagued him for a year was liver cancer. We walked one afternoon in early March to his allotment overlooking the grounds of Forty Hall in north London and then into Gough Woods to see what birds were there. He was slow already. His scalp was patchy with alopecia. His abdomen was bloated and tender. His pockets as usual were full of acorns. We heeled them into the ground in hedgerows where elm disease had destroyed the trees. We were oaking the landscape. Dad had always planted acorns, even before elm disease. It was not a mission. He heeled them in without any introspection. The sports club where he had been groundsman had – still has – a stockade of oaks, some more than thirty years old by then, from acorns which Dad had dropped or thrown. The Essex, Middlesex, Hertfordshire borders where he had walked for years can thank him for a thousand trees.

We hardly mentioned illness. We looked for birds – and saw a pair of woodcock – and talked about the news that day that the Liverpool grave-diggers had called off the strike that had prevented so many burials during Jim Callaghan's Winter of Discontent. Dad was not a sentimentalist. He wouldn't want his corpse to cross a picket line. But as a Labour Party member he acknowledged the electoral damage that would be caused by the unburied dead, and the uncollected rubbish in the streets, the unheated schools, the strike-hit hospitals. The Tories were already 20 per cent ahead in the opinion polls – but we were optimists, expecting only socialism and cancer cures. I kept a good, strong, orange acorn for myself. I did not heel it in, but put it in my anorak to dry. A worry bead for Dad. I only had to finger it each day and Dad would soon be well. Except the acorn was forgotten, never touched or rubbed until it was too late. And by then, of course, that acorn had been lost.

In the following days, not depressed at all, I flew from Plymouth to Jersey in a Twin Otter, from Manston to Brussels in a Piper Chieftain, from Alderney to Shoreham in an Islander, from Glasgow to Tiree in a Trilander. I tested the world's shortest scheduled service

– between Westray and Papa Westray in the Orkneys, a 90-second flight over a distance shorter than Heathrow's runway. I landed on Barra's tidal sand in the Hebrides. It's safe to land when the lady in the tea hut can see the paddling seagulls' legs.

Airlines opened and closed by the day. Air Wales – running out of Cardiff to Chester – folded the moment I booked my seat. Air Westward was grounded hours before I was due to take its flight from Exeter to Glasgow. But, the following week, Air Kent was taxi-ing for take-off on its first flight, for Rotterdam – and I was there, aboard the ten-seater Port of Ramsgate, depressed and for the first time in my life fearful in the air. My surgeons research had led me to a pioneer in liver transplants, Professor Roy Calne of Addenbrooke's in Cambridge, and to the plain-speaking medical jour-nalist Donald Gould. I mentioned to both a patient of my acquaintance, a Londoner of sixty-seven, a bird-watcher, a socialist, a planter of trees, whose ulcer had turned out to be a cancer of the liver. 'His doctors say they'll give him drugs to shrink the tumour,' I said, seeking confirmation for our optimism. Professor Calne, the liver expert, knew of no such procedures. And Donald Gould? He said, 'Nonsense. The doctors are kidding the patient because they know he'll die. A liver tumour can't be shrunk.' Except he was more blunt than that. I had a flight to catch. I contemplated my father's death at low altitudes above a choppy sea. I'd never been so airborne in my life.

At Whitsun we were camping in Cornwall in a field above the Logan Rock at Treen when the message came – via the village shop – that Dad was dying and that I should hurry to London. He could not walk or talk. We fixed him up with a sheepskin, to ease his bed sores, and a bedside bell so that he could call for help. The bell went all night long. I had to lift his penis into a grey cardboard bottle so that he could try – and fail – to urinate. I had to shave his face. I had to scrape the anchovies of damp wax from his blocked ears – just as he had done for me so many times when I was a child.

On Sunday June 3rd he seemed to rally. We carried him as best we could into the garden so that he could feel the sun, but this resurrection was short-lived. He soon was unconscious, only waking for the pain. On the Tuesday he went into a local hospital and there, in the small hours of the Wednesday morning, he died, alone. He did not want a funeral service. He didn't care for priests or prayers or hymns. No flowers. No grief. Immediate family only. He did not want his ashes scattered anywhere. We let the crematorium dispose of him, and spent his wake disposing of his papers and his clothes. His allotment trousers were too old for Oxfam. I put them in the bin, but searched the pockets first. I found his wooden-handled pruning knife (which I still have and use) and half a dozen acorns. One day I'd find the proper place to heel them in. Instead of tears I shed my first piece of fiction for many years: a monologue by a woman whose father is dying called 'Seven Ages'.

It was published by Craig Raine in *Quarto* and then broadcast on Radio 3, and marked the start of my migration from journalism to fiction. The last lines were: 'If Father goes, then what? Who is there left? Who is next in line? A foolish idea comes into my mind as I sit at the end of his bed: to turn my head and have him scrape the wax from my ear. More and more I am victim to such unexpected sentiments. Of course, I keep them to myself. This is no time for self-pity – though, sometimes, I wonder what has become of my good fortune.' That was the year that we swapped Thatcher for my Dad.

In late December I was in the air again. I flew up to Skye from Glasgow in a draughty, baby-Fiat of an aircraft, with bird-lime burns in its paintwork, to interview Ian Anderson of the rock group Jethro Tull. In his new incarnation as Laird of Straithaird, he was replanting the profits of his flute back into 15,300 acres of his virtually treeless Skye estate. I had Dad's acorns in my coat – and was still looking for some sentimental place to bury them. It occurred to me that I should plant them there and then, on Skye. But this was private property, and Dad had always oaked the public land.

I took the flight back south. 'We've made rather a speciality of taking writers back home,' the pilot said, once he'd learned my occupation. 'We run a Coffin Charter. We take the writers home to be buried. We took Compton MacKenzie back to Barra. And we also took Eric Linklater back to Orkney.' It was a fearful journey with 35-knot headwinds labouring against the plane, its wings hardly able to locate soft passage in the dusk. I am more introspective – and more theatrical – than Dad ever was. I dropped his acorns somewhere over Argyll, but the wind might have scattered them in Orkney and beyond. We made the slowest progress one can make by air and, robbed of acorns, bereft of my good fortune, I feared that I would never reach the ground. Physically I did, an hour overdue. But, otherwise, I never touched the ground again, not solidly, not after 1979. Since then I seem to spend the whole time in the air, gliding in the gusty thermals of my father's death. There is no gravestone, no ashy earth, to take a bearing from. But there are oaks.

CANDIA McWILLIAM

1980

ASKED TO CHOOSE, from a list of specified years, and to describe a year in my life, I have come up hard against the innumeracy of my memory, which seems to pour out information from its leaky pockets when stimulated by fear or boredom, but to keep nothing in its files labelled by year, save the perennial tics and preoccupations that I do not need my memory to tell me were there.

Since I am fond of the illusion of another chance, I like new years although I do not much care for New Year; the childish longing to hear a great page turn in the sky has not left me, but all there is to hear is beating time. For much of our lives we can deafen ourselves to it, but at New Year we concentrate upon it and listen for its greater theme, which seems to me at the winter's sunk heart to be preponderantly sad. Since we can only live up to time when we are not conscious of it, I am grateful when the second day of the new year comes and shows itself to have much in common with the last day of the old.

At the beginning of 1980 I was twenty-five, living in London and working as a copywriter in a small advertising agency. Everything about the job was unlike the idea we have now in the 1990s of an advertising agency in the 1980s, which had not, in their most satirized sense, begun to bite. I worked for a committed

Liberal (the only and last Liberal on the Greater London Council), a musician and a startling mimic who encouraged jokes and whose favourite accounts were charities. Pragmatically Robin Hood-like, he had several remunerative though not huge clients, some of them wishing to sell challengingly unappealing things. It was a happy office and I liked the job more than any I had had, so I am glad to have a souvenir of one of the items that proved impossible to shift.

Many bewildering gadgets without visible attraction were bought in their thousands thanks to the prestidigitation of the Art Director and a few choice words from us. A brown fur-fabric pyjama case of about a yard long, all but rigid and equipped with eyes and whiskers, stole my heart, and for it I wrote (for printing in a magazine with a considerable circulation) 'Here is an Otter you Can't Refuse'. One otter was sold, and my children have it still.

For the Spar group of supermarkets, we toiled over the entire language and extracted the words, for display on carrier bags and other company livery material, 'So near, so Spar'. I was sorry to leave the job; they were no doubt quite reconciled to seeing me go, since I had been receiving highly disruptive telephone calls from the boat on which the man to whom I was engaged was, as was his habit, crossing an ocean. It is not easy to disguise from clients that the call one is taking in their meeting is ship-to-shore through Portishead when one has to shout 'Over' at the end of every remark.

In late April, he flew home from the Pacific, which he had crossed under sail, having passed through the Panama Canal, from Colon (where he was chased by gunmen from the shores of Contadora, where he had simply intended to picnic, not knowing that the Shah was dying there) to Tahiti via the Galápagos and the Marquesas, to collect me. I was to have a taste of the sea. I had sailed, timidly, reluctantly, but with some frequency, in the changeable waters of lochs and the Scots Atlantic. I had seen the Corryvreckan and been overboard, though not there, among seals and mackerel. I knew many of the right nautical words (which can waterlog a writer more swiftly than almost any other 'flavoured' vocabulary). A twenty-three-language dictionary for yachtsmen lay on my childhood mantelpiece; I would sometimes surprise people by knowing the Swedish for 'clinker built'.

None of it helped. We flew to Tahiti via Los Angeles where I was kept under guard because I had forgotten to get an American visa. The guards were armed and polite not in the manner of villains but of zookeepers. In Tahiti, where we arrived at three o'clock in the morning, there were more guards, including, true to tropical thriller form, a tough uniformed Frenchwoman, with waist-length hair and a machine gun, who accompanied me to the lavatory while my companion tried to explain that we would not in any way attempt to take benefits or monies from the French State and that we would soon be leaving this paradise where a can of Coca Cola cost, then, two pounds.

The boat was 'parked', stern to, on the main boulevard of Tahiti's capital, Papeete. One side of the street, planted with oleander and frangipani and signposts, is fitted out as a mooring. You can walk off your gangplank and cross the road for a croissant. Yet Papeete was not an idyllic town. It was too commercial for idyll. Many of the people are beautiful and they are all dressed in a way that is admirably becoming and democratic, in a piece of cloth called a *pareo*, usually flowered, wound about the body. Men and women wear flowers in their hair and some of the loveliest women are not women at all but *ré-rés* – boys who have been raised as girls because daughters are so much prized. This instinctive fairness of spirit survives within a system of colonial government that is efficient, officious, bureaucratic and expensive. Almost everything is imported, much of it from France. French culinary chauvinism brings many delicacies, though well-travelled Camembert hot off the Nouméa–Papeete ferry is not one of them.

There is a charming as well as an oppressive side to this, but the unavoidable impression of Tahiti is of a paradise smirched. Until one is out of the town it is hard to sense the freedom the place offered Gauguin. One's trite expectations of its physical beauty are amply gratified, but instead of decontracted ease its atmosphere is to a considerable extent one of frustration and resentment. The damage done by missionaries and tourism is rawly evident. Somehow, Tahiti has become a place it is pleasant to leave, although as you leave you begin to reassemble your memories of it, leaving out what is mean and consolidating what has not been and cannot be spoilt.

In Papeete, moored next to the boat on which we were to live at sea for the next months, was a small yacht called *Joshua*. She had been made for one of the sea's most honoured sailors, Bernard Moitessier, who was to be seen daily, attending to the minute practicalities of maintaining his craft, taking water on board, returning from shopping with a net of big pale green Pacific grapefruit. *Joshua* was without anything inessential. Idling at the urban dockside among longer, fatter, sleeker vessels carrying great wardrobes of sail and studded and bristling with dials, sonar, radar, satellite navigation, she and her slight, silver-haired skipper were regarded with awe and visited constantly by admiring gazers, looking rather like inhabitants of Palm Beach come to see St Jerome and his lion. Her small metal deck was punctuated by carefully placed handles, for Moitessier to grip as he adjusted, or took down, her canvas in a big sea. *Joshua* has been round Cape Horn the wrong way; she and Moitessier are legends of skill and courage. Together they seemed to express the best of what is simple in a place uncomfortable with and yet dependent upon the world's sophistications.

The society of those who live at sea has its own systems, signals and secret recognitions. Hanging off the tall, toothed, purple island of Moorea we met a couple whose children's school was the radio and whose

Dalmatian was afraid of the solid feel of dry land. We met several people (all whites) in flight from South Africa and a number of undaunted Americans in their seventies who had escaped their lives and their things and were living lightly. Australians and New Zealanders, who could fix anything and owned nothing, worked their way around and around the world in big boats on their good nature and hard hearts. They were invariably blond from the salt, and shed burnt skin as casually as they spawned kids. From time to time a maverick, a lone sailor in a boat the size of a canoe, would be rumoured to be about in an anchorage. While we were there, besides the heroic Moitessier, there was a boy who had crossed the Atlantic in a boat shorter than he was tall, living on raw porridge oats mixed with olive oil.

Our boat was a beauty but no grace holds off the sea, or cockroaches. By the time we had passed through the Society Islands and were set on course for Tonga, the untinned food (stored under bunks; no space is unused on a boat, it is packed like an egg) smacked of the roach repellent Baygon, and we had had some bleak squalls that rose and sank with a speed and violence that kept us continually wary. I was more frightened by the occasional rasp of coral on the anchor chain if we were hanging off an atoll by night. The fragility of the boat, its gay vanity, made me think of Hardy's poem, intentionally at the same time meretricious and moving, 'The Convergence of the Twain'.

Tonga is an archipelago whose capital, Nuku'alofa, is on the main island. The Tongans, out of respect for their king who lives in a white clapboard palace rather like a house in *Couples*, wear a rolled length of thick woven grass that often reaches to below the knees. Following the royal example (although I read in 1992 that King Tonga Tupu has been slimming), they are a substantial people. They were almost menacingly hospitable and anxious to take me home for a proper meal cooked in an *umu* or underground oven. More than once a wide Chevy or Dodge would pull up and its driver slowly emerge, already tall and dressed in the then fashionable platform soles, to tower over me (I am six feet tall, and not skinny) and bewail my scrawniness. This unfamiliar approach combined with the treesful of flying foxes, a good, dusty, secondhand bookshop and a Chinese restaurant apparently built in honour of Chiang Kai Shek but delicious none the less, to give Tonga a charm that was less glamorous than that of Bora Bora, for example, but also better for condensation into stories, which become essential to people living on the watch system, four hours on, four hours off. What was sad about Tonga was true of all the islands of any size that we came upon; the stranglehold of the Church of Jesus Christ and the Latter Day Saints. It is a relief to contemplate the sites of orgy and human sacrifice after encountering example after example of these well-regulated interference posts.

In Tonga I bought a book by Joan Didion (*Run,*

River, which I fell upon in gratitude for its nerviness amid the literal, physically demanding life I was leading) and an Arden Press *Antony and Cleopatra*. When, later, we passed through what I thought was certain death (a hurricane, north of New Zealand), I read the play round and round, unsleeping, through four dog watches, as though it were prayer. I trusted the power of the words more than I trusted the fabric of the boat as the water covered us again and again.

I fell into the harbour at Nuku'alofa, which is unlike most harbours in the South Pacific, not being aflash with bright fish nor grazed by blue-lipped clams, though I am sure it shelters many moray eels, those energetic toothed thews of killer muscle. I had missed my balance on a thwart of the tender in a swell, clad in a daft bit of blue silk. In the dirty harbour water floated a yellow plastic bag with on it the, suddenly nostalgic, words 'So near, so Spar'.

JULIAN BARNES

1981

R.P. Fleury, Brittany, 1967

D ON'T TALK TO ME about Janis Joplin, Jim Morrison, Brian Jones, Jimi Hendrix, that lost Beach
Boy, or any of the lesser pop-rock deaths. I get no
necrothrill from a drug overdose, a stoned slump into
the void glorified as 'life at the edge', an episode of
melodramatic self-indulgence inflated into the greatest
loss to the musical world since the early death of
Schubert. (Oh, and can we settle that Keats versus
Dylan conundrum? Keats was the better poet, Dylan
the better rock musician.) No, the three deaths I prefer
to hymn are sourly ordinary deaths, dragging hospital
terminations of the kind more likely to await the rest of
us: heart disease, cancer, cancer. Boris Vian on 23 June
1959, Jacques Brel on 9 October 1978, and finally
Georges Brassens on 29 October 1981 at 23h 15 precisely. That was the moment at which French song –
Francophone song, to be exact, since Brel was Belgian
– died for me; or at least stopped being interesting.

I spent the academic year of 1966–7 teaching as a
lecteur d'anglais (the slightly posher term for *assistant*) at
the Collège Saint-Martin in Rennes. My task was to
instruct my pupils in 'English conversation and English
civilization', which in turn meant devising various strat-
egies to keep them quiet and avoid the glowering
irruption into the classroom of the *surveillant général*, an
ex-Algerian War veteran who terrified me even more

93

than he did the boys. Some of my pupils, by means of diligently failing the *baccalauréat* and being sent back to retake it, were almost the same age as me, and certainly more sophisticated. I'm not sure how reliably English civilization was depicted in our conversations – I remember being grilled about London night-clubs (I bluffed tremendously) and London girls (ditto); though I would become more plausibly authoritative on the key cultural question of that time, whether or not the Beatles would break up. More benefit probably flowed in the opposite direction. Living among priests I became familiar with the kindlier side of the Catholic religion; eating at the school I found that roast beef came in other hues than field-marshal grey; and in my solitude I was enriched and consoled by the discovery of French song.

For about two-thirds of that year the top of the French hit-parade was squatted on by 'A Whiter Shade Of Pale', that haunting confection from Procul Harum. But the singers who roared from my squeaky French player with a stylus-weight of about two kilos were all local: Brassens and Brel, Vian and Reggiani; high-boho Léo Ferré, pointedly engagé Jean Ferrat, soufflée-voiced Ingénieur des Ponts et Chaussées Guy Béart, lugubrious Anne Vanderlove, bouncy Georges Chelon, yearning Barbara, chubbily smutty Pierre Perret, winsome Anne Sylvestre, and promising Rennes-born débutant Jacques Bertin. I gave a polite nod to earlier generations (Piaf, Trenet, Rossi), a shrug to the international cabaret artists (Aznavour, Distel, the ear-cupping Bécaud), a pained smile to that Hayley Mills of *chanson* Françoise Hardy, and a sneer to the home-grown *yéyé*-mongers, Hallyday, Claude François and Eddy Mitchell. ('Clo-Clo' had at least kept his own name: Mitchell began life as the priestly sounding Claude Moine, Hallyday as the distinctly unrockerish Jean-Philippe Smet. On the other hand, 'Clo-Clo' made up for this with a spectacularly unstylish death, involving the bath, electricity and, it was rumoured, a minority sexual practice.

Procul Harum's line-up changed even before their song became a hit, and its less than cogent words were penned by Nobody Remembers Whom. Most of the singers I admired, by contrast, were individualists who wrote or co-wrote their own stuff; while some owned the whole aesthetic means of production and were badged with the lordly initials 'ACI' – *auteur-compositeur-interprète*. The three who have accompanied me most down the years, their poppy, fizzing vinyl surfaces finally traded up to CD, are Boris Vian, Jacques Brel and Georges Brassens. All three had emerged during the early fifties, when they were first recorded by Jacques Canetti, brother of the Nobel-winning Elias. Vian, wry and urbane, sang at the world with a cutting edge of sardonic disbelief. Brel, urgent and impassioned, sang at the world as if it could have sense shaken into it by music, could be saved from its follies and brutalities by his vocal embrace. Brassens, intimate and formal, sang at the world as if it were an old lover whose ways are teasingly familiar and from whom not too much is expected. Vian died at thirty-nine; Brel at forty-nine; Brassens, in a final act of non-conformity, just managed to stagger past fifty-nine.

Many of the singers I listened to expressed a vibrant anti-clericalism; but the indulgent Père Fleury in the next cell only complained at the volume of secular ranting when he was in the middle of confessing a pupil. Most of the Fathers treated my atheism – like my nationality, my long hair and my austerity in the face of wine – as something basically odd but tolerable. Père Marais, one of the more ironical and inflammatory priests (who fondly remembered London bus-conductors shortening 'Thank you' to 'Kew') used to apostrophize me with an amused eye: 'You just wait for the next world, you civilians, then we clergy will show you who's going to be saved. You may have the upper hand now but later on you're going to be in the shit.' Père de Goësbriand, from an aristocratic Breton family, who was much teased for having been shot in the left buttock during the war ('Running away, Hubert?' 'We were surrounded!'), overheard me arguing one day with Père Marais, and afterwards voiced his anxiety: if I hadn't been baptized, he pointed out, then I had no soul and hadn't a prayer of getting to Heaven. He was much preoccupied with this final destination; on another occasion, he admitted with a confidential wink, 'Of course, you don't think I'd put up with all this if there wasn't Heaven in it for me at the end, do you?'

The physics teacher, Père Daumer, a fleshy, hip-heavy, hairless man who was never out of his cassock (his nickname among the pupils was 'The Third Sex') also displayed moral concern for me. After I had been in residence a few weeks, he took me aside and explained that some of the words I was hearing over meals at my end of the refectory table were vulgar and not repeatable in polite conversation. I, in return, worried about Père Daumer, who despite a severe conservatism in religious matters was a devotee of films on television, and was thus obliged to wade through a lot of soul-tarnishing stuff: Godard's *A Bout de souffle* had aroused his particular disapproval. However, such was his cinematic passion that he would doggedly stay in the fag-fogged TV room until the credits. Then he would rise and pronounce judgement before going off to bed. 'Not worth the trouble' was a favourite verdict. Once, to my delight, he gave some piece of sinful froth the full treatment. 'Lacking both interest *and* morality,' he remarked, doffing his little square black cap at me. 'Bonsoir, Monsieur Barnes.'

There was considerable doctrinal disagreement in this house of Eudistes. Not from Père Calvard, an ardent Breton patriot who managed to combine Druidism and Catholicism with no ideological difficulty; nor from the football-mad Père Le Mauff, who would briskly assert 'Metaphysics is rubbish' before going off to tend his hive of bees, his broken-winged buzzard, his month-old fox-cub. The dispute was the sempiternal one between Ancients and Moderns, and embraced

97

teaching methods as much as beliefs. Père Tupin, a young firebrand who believed in 'dialogue' with pupils, and would even discuss masturbation with them, had recently got into trouble with the authorities for taking as his text for sermon the words of a pop song. (He got into trouble with me over this too, since to my amazement he hadn't chosen Brel or Brassens but a piece of dreck warbled by someone like Sylvie Vartan.) Presiding over these theologically sultry days at the Collège was Père Denis, a Père Supérieur renowned for his fairminded timidity, his desire to approve of most things he set eyes on, and a certain tentativeness in conversation. Père Marais used to recall at frequent intervals – and always with undiminished glee – an outing with the Père Supérieur and one of my predecessors as *lecteur d'anglais*. At one point they had passed a dog. 'Tell me, Monsieur Smith,' the Superior had asked with an exact civility. 'Do you have dogs in England?'

I like to remember that Boris Vian was one of the amplified voices with which I used to blast Père Fleury (who dodged behind trees when he saw a nun approaching, and who also rolled the fattest gaspers I have ever seen, each requiring two full cigarette papers). But this must be a false memory. Vian's fame as an interpreter didn't really begin until 1979, twenty years after his death, when Philips released a commemorative LP. In 1966–7 he was known through the voices of others: Serge Reggiani had begun his career performing Vian's work; Peter, Paul and Mary made a transatlantic campus heart-plucker out of 'The Deserter'; and Jean Ferrat had offered up his smokey-jazz homage 'Boris'. Vian was remembered instead as everything except an interpreter: song-writer, poet, novelist, playwright, translator, actor, jazz trumpeter, pataphysician. He was the most cosmopolitan of my top three: his photo-biography begins with him standing, aged twelve, behind a big chubby boy in long shorts and a criss-cross sweater who turns out to be Yehudi Menuhin; later we see him with his arm round Miles Davis, chatting to Ellington, meeting Errol Garner at Orly airport in 1957; here he is on the beach at Antibes and Saint Tropez, behind the wheel of his Aston Martin, his Morgan, his 1911 Brazier; on film he lurks in the shadows with Jeanne Moreau in the Vadim version of *Les Liaisons dangereuses*. He wrote songs with Aznavourian profligacy: over 700 of them, some jazz-influenced, some in the style of *rock humoristique* that he pioneered with Henri Salvador. Despite 'Le Déserteur', he didn't write 'protest songs' so much as songs of satirical provocation, anarchic moralities like 'Le Petit commerce', which laments the plight of an arms salesman so successful that all his clients kill one another off and reduce him to penury. In his lifetime Vian wasn't held to be a convincing interpreter of his own work, but the 1979 Philips disc gives the lie to this: his ironic, whippy-tongued delivery was the apt match for his sly and worldly songs.

So Vian was necessarily for later. In 1966–7 it was Jacques Brel who spoke most directly, publicly and intimately to the twenty-year-old I then was. While British rockers strutted their pit-bull masculinity, Brel sang of sexual hurt and romantic humiliation; while Distel smarmed on about *luuurv*, Brel exalted *la tendresse*. In other moods he gleefully spanked the bourgeoisie, lobbed grenades at the military, wrangled doggedly with God, and sang about death with a vibrant terror which seemed to replicate my own. Yet even when he agreed with you, he saw further: his rousing war-cry 'Les Bourgeois' ('c'est comme les cochons/Plus ça devient vieux, plus ça devient bête') turns out in its final verse to be a sager comment on the whole inevitable process of *embourgeoisement*, with youthful mockers transformed into middle-aged mockees. It was Brel's mixture of satire, wisdom and heart that did for me: alongside the snarl and the lush contempt was a bursting emotionalism, a celebration of love as *la tendre guerre*, an aching sympathy for the weak, the lost, the *amputés de coeur*. This Belgian came out of a cold, flat, wet country, yet sang with such heat; he hurled himself with dangerous directness at his audience, not caring whose toes he stepped on, acting and clowning, playing drunks and simpletons, even doing sheep-noises, but bundling you up in that rich gargly tonsilly voice and whirling you round in his thrilling gibes and joyous dreams.

Today he is dead – buried at Altuona a few metres away from Gauguin – and his musical remains sit on the shelf in a cube of ten CDs: smaller than the box you'd get someone's ashes in. Playing through this whole *oeuvre* again, I am struck by how long it took him (compared to Brassens, say) to find his true musical identity. His early songs are weakened by sentimentality and preachiness: not for nothing was he teased as 'l'Abbé Brel'. (He had had a late-adolescent brush with muscular Christianity, and we should always beware the lapsed evangelist.) He strains for poeticality, has a taste for moody townscapes, and offers a routine view of girls and love which often has a drab tang of misogyny (it's hard to think of a more charm-free description of an ex-lover than the phrase 'matériel déclassé' from 'La Haine'). The moral thumpiness is heightened by the use of organ and backing choir, not to mention the spoken *ex cathedra* pronouncement. A typical song of this early period is 'Prière païenne', a pious attempt to convince the Virgin Mary that carnal love is pretty much a metaphorical equivalent of spiritual love. Mary, if listening, might have given a sceptical pout.

Once Brel has wriggled free of these beginnings and sorted out his orchestration (high whiney strings like the complaining *vent du nord*, snarly brass, whizzy accordion), he drove his way to a short yet wonderfully rich creative peak, lasting from about 1961 to 1967. He sang of the north, of getting drunk (in the north), of sexual betrayal (and getting drunk, as a result, in the north), of being widowed (and discovering, on the day of the funeral, that you have been sexually betrayed, and therefore getting drunk – probably in the north – as a result). He sang exactly of childhood's yearnings, of the pursuit and loss of *le Far-West*. He sang what must be the only song in general currency inspired by the queue for a military brothel. He sang ragingly of 'adult' foolishness ('Il nous fallut bien du talent/Pour être vieux sans être adultes') and mockingly of the old man's death he was never to know. He sang funeral laments for his friends ('Jojo', 'Fernand') which now have to double in our listening as elegies for him too. In his maturity he could still be merely contrary (as in the puckishly anti-ruralist 'Les Moutons', which begins 'Désolé bergère/ J'aime pas les moutons'); but it is his understanding of the complication and weak starting-point of most human dealings that gives his work its strength and continuing life. 'On se croit mèche, on n'est que suif' (We think we are the wick, but we are only the tallow). We dream of going to sea – and end up as captain of a breakwater. Logically, the source of all this imperfection must be imperfect Himself:

> *Moi, si j'étais le bon Dieu*
> *Je crois que je serais pas fier*
> *Je sais, on fait ce qu'on peut,*
> *Mais y a la manière.*

'Lacking both interest *and* morality,' Père Daumer would doubtless have said, doffing his black cap.

While I was in France Brel made his sole appearance in Britain (Brassens visited us just once as well); and in 1967 came the announcement – far more catastrophic than any Beatles break-up – that he was retiring, or at least abandoning his *tours de chant*. Unlike those indefatigable retirees whose valedictory appearances are an annual event on several continents, Brel said he would give up, and he did. His energy went instead into films and musicals, travel and his new Polynesian life. Though he was to record a final album a decade later, his public recitals were over. But first he came to Rennes.

I knew nothing about him except that he was Belgian, slim, dark, and horse-toothed; that he smoked too much and knew how to pilot light aircraft. Most of this information was drawn from the sumptuous folding album covers of Disques Barclay. I didn't want to know more either. The songs were the man; any biography was unimportant, reductive. Who cared if there was a real Marieke or Mathilde or Madeleine behind 'Marieke' and 'Mathilde' and 'Madeleine'? When Olivier Todd's posthumous *Jacques Brel: Une Vie* came out, I duly read it, and was duly disappointed: not by the discovery that Brel was a good bit more imperfect than his songs, but by a biographer who had begun in sympathy and ended in nagging disapproval, his enthusiasm for the work diminished by his knowledge of the man. It was little compensation to make the occasional *trouvaille*: for instance, that 'La Valse à mille temps' had its moment of origin when Brel was driving towards Tangier from the mountains, and discovered in the rhythm of the road's innumerable bends the surging acceleration of a waltz.

It was a hot evening, even hotter up in the gallery. The show began at about ten with Brel's regular warm-up act, a black American group called the Delta Rhythm Boys, who were doubtless very good but seemed to me interminable. I was sleepy and hungry by the time – nearing midnight – that Brel came on stage, yet all was instantly forgiven. A minimal band (piano, drums, bass, accordion) and no fancy lighting or presentation. After the first song, he took off his jacket ('Ça chauffe, hein?'). The audience never once clapped in self-applauding recognition at the start of a song; even the intros had become precious. Of course, I knew most of the songs already from disc, so the words came from within me as well as from the stage, in that haunting stereo of memory and the real moment. Down there, on that familiar equine face, the sweat famously poured: Brel was said to lose 800g during a recital. He hurtled straight from one song into the next, without a pause, without any colluding chat, for an hour, then brusquely stopped. And that was it – no encores, no showbiz, no lachrymose farewell. He left us without ceremony.

Brel had the romantic presence, the newsworthy life, the concentrated burst of albums. Brassens had a reputation as *un ours*, was publicly reticent, and assembled his work slowly but persistently over thirty years, with a quiet tenacity appropriate to the son and grandson of stonemasons. He was more classical in style than Brel, and more literary (he had even tried to write fiction). He looked and sounded like a sage from a hill-village, but in fact had never lived in the country and said he would be a naturalized Parisian if such a thing were possible. He sang with a growling, chestnut voice, with a rolling Provençal *r*, with a crisp, humorous delivery. For all the jollity and disruptiveness of his texts, his sound always remained austere. His maximum orchestration consisted of a second guitar and a double bass, both as discreet as the confessional. There is a moment in 'La Non-demande en mariage' when the bass – after fifteen years of chuntering away quietly in the background – comes loping in with a loud and insistently held contribution. It registers seismically with the listener.

The Brassens canon, as it struck successive generations from the fifties onwards, was warming and freeing. He was an anarchist: not so much a political one (though he had been a member of the Fédération d'Anarchistes at the end of the war), still less a hippified one, but a genuine and unpretentious free spirit. He was a man of the people, though not a man of the crowd, and his songs display an even-handed disdain for all organizers of society regardless of political persuasion. He mistrusted the group, believing that as soon as there are more than four of you, you become a *bande de cons* ('Le Pluriel'); he detested all uniforms 'except that of the postman'; and seems to have had a sociopathic hatred for *chefs de gare*. Like Vian and Brel he wrote anti-militaristic songs, but his hatred of war did not find predictable expression: see, for instance, his jaunty consumers' report on the subject ('Moi, mon colon, cell' que j'préfère/C'est la guerr' de quatorz'-dix-huit!'). His unpolite mockery of most sensible preconceptions about life was the more bracing – if initially puzzling – for being allied to a code of charity, pleasure and humour.

He celebrated the downtrodden: cowards, pimps, gravediggers, tarts with ordinary hearts, women with huge arses, traitors, shaven-headed collaborationists, older women (as I get older myself I increasingly treasure his line from 'Saturne' – 'Et la petite pisseuse d'en face/Peut bien aller se rehabiller'). He was on the side of the solitary pyromaniac against the combined forces of the *sapeurs pompiers*; he saluted the man who had burgled his house (arguing that since the burglar got what he wanted, and he, Brassens, had derived a song from the incident, then the two of them were quits). He praised cats, pipes, male comradeship, and the artichoke-hearted woman who gives everyone a leaf. He execrated judges, gendarmes, right-thinking people, and the heartlessly principled. Yet his tenderness could be robust, and enemies were not always forgiven. In the mid-sixties, Brassens visibly lost weight, shrinking from an ursine presence towards comparative gauntness. Journalists informed their readers that the great singer had cancer. Their speculations were true; but though true, none the less intrusive. Brassens responded with 'Le Bulletin de santé', in which he admits that he has indeed left the ranks of the obese, but not for the reasons some impute. No – *non, non, non, trois fois non* –

what has caused him to lose so much weight is not illness but the fact that he has spent a vast amount of time and energy fucking journalists' wives. Not the most delicate riposte, perhaps, but the provocation was hardly delicate either. And just to emphasize the aggressive corporeality of the matter, Brassens filches Mallarmé's line 'Je suis hanté: l'Azur, l'Azur, l'Azur, l'Azur!' and twists it into 'Je suis hanté: le rut, le rut, le rut, le rut!'

In 'Le Mauvais sujet repenti', one of his earliest songs (1953), Brassens takes on the voice of a pimp (or at least a semi-pro) to discuss the training-up of a débutante tart's sexual gift:

> L'avait l' don, c'est vrai, j'en conviens,
> L'avait le génie,
> Mais, sans technique, un don n'est rien
> Qu'un' sal' manie . . .

Without technique, a gift – even one amounting to genius – is no more than a quirky habit. (A note on the social penetration of Brassens's work: three decades and more later, when Jacques Fouroux was preparing the French rugby team to face the New Zealanders, he observed that 'pour reprendre la formule de Brassens: le talent sans technique n'est qu'une sale manie'.) Despite – or perhaps because of – his restricted range of possible sound, Brassens throughout his career was constantly elaborating his technique, inventing, tautening, broadening: across three decades his ballads get grander, his melodies denser, his repeat-schemes more intricate.

Thematically, his songs complicate too, as his understanding of the world complicates. In his early work, sex is a jolly and frequently satirical business, in which adultery is an act of cheerful revenge, escaped gorillas have their way with robed judges, and genial fetishists are obsessed with the belly-buttons of policemen's wives. In maturity, Brassens is more likely to hymn the Penelope who strays, the adulterer who can only perform if he really likes the husband he's cuckolding, and the poignant position ('Ma Maîtresse, La Traîtresse') of the lover who feels betrayed when his mistress chooses to sleep with her husband. The singer is also quite happy to insult his compatriots' self-image as lovers whose silky skills unfailingly provoke seamless ecstasy: 'Quatre-Vingt Quinze Pour Cent', according to him, is the percentage of women who are faking it. But then Brassens never pleased by seeking to please. Another statistic: in 1977 a survey suggested that 64.7 per cent of the French would like to be in his skin because for them he represented The Happy Man. Asked to comment, he replied, 'Ah, les cons . . .'

The Collège Saint-Martin at Rennes was where I saw my first dead body: that of Père Roussel, a young priest who had succumbed in his twenties to some ungodly disease. He was laid out in a vestibule off the entrance hall to the main building, and boys were encouraged to visit him and pray for his soul. I drew the line at this, though gazed through the windowed doors at the pallid, bespectacled figure lying on his back.

Upstairs I listened to Brel satirically discussing his own death in 'Tango Funèbre' and in 'Le Moribond':

> *Et je veux qu'on rie*
> *Je veux qu'on danse*
> *Je veux qu'on s'amuse comme des fous*
> *Je veux qu'on rie*
> *Je veux qu'on danse*
> *Quand c'est qu'on me mettra dans mon trou*

As for Brassens, the album that he brought out during my year in Rennes – *Georges Brassens IX* – began with an enormous departure for this established master of the two-, three-, or if you were very lucky four-minute ballad. 'Supplique pour être enterré sur la plage de Sète' weighs in at a marathon seven minutes and eighteen seconds. It is a grand, lilting, jocular codicil to his earlier testamentary songs, and contains specific instruction for the disposal of his body. He wants it transported 'dans un sleeping du Paris-Mediterranée' to the 'minuscule' station at Sète (where the *chef de gare* would probably have the delicacy to give himself the day off), and thence to the beach for burial. The eternal *estivant* is to lie in the sun between sky and sea, spending his death on holiday. He hopes that girls will undress behind his tomb; perhaps one of them will even stretch out on the sand in the shadow of his cross – thus affording his spirit 'un petit bonheur posthume'. And just as Brel in Altuona was to have Gauguin for company, at Sète Brassens would be close to Paul Valéry, delineator and occupant of *Le Cimetière marin*. The singer, a humble troubadour beside the great poet, would at least be able to congratulate himself that 'Mon cimetière soit plus marin que le sien'.

In the event, he didn't quite make the beach; instead, on the first weekend of November 1981, he was added to the family vault in what had formerly been the paupers' graveyard. (This despite complaining in the 'Supplique' that the vault was already stuffed to bursting point and he didn't want to be reduced to shouting 'Move along inside there please' – 'Place aux jeunes en quelque sorte'.) The ending of his life contained the symmetry he desired and feared: born in Sète in 1921, the naturalized Parisian returned to die there sixty years later. In that shortened span he never travelled well himself (being allergic to aeroplanes and abroad), while his songs, with their compacted, allusive, slangy texts and spare music, have travelled less successfully than those of Brel. But he was France's greatest and wisest singer, and we should visit him – spending his death on holiday – in whatever way we can.

CLIVE JAMES

1982

Koo Stark captured by paparazzi

I t was the only year I ever thought of at the time as being a special year by itself, so it's the only one I can look back on with any sure recollection as to its events. Other years interchange their events in memory. When I was writing the first draft of the television series *Fame in the Twentieth Century*, I worked from memory, and found out only while checking for the next draft that I had continually got things out of order. Memory rearranges even the biggest, world-scale happenings into a more manageable sequence. Memory edits. Memory would have edited 1982 if, before the year began, I hadn't persuaded Karl Miller of the *London Review of Books* to serialize an *ottava rima* verse chronicle which would treat the year's news as it came, with no benefit of hindsight. It was typically generous of Miller to be attracted by this prospect, because there was no guarantee that much of interest would actually happen.

And at first, indeed, everything seemed drearily normal. General Jaruzelski, ruling Poland, rounded up all the Solidarity activists and penned them in the open air while the snow fell. As things went in the East, nothing could be more humdrum than that. Roy Jenkins stood for the Glasgow seat of Hillhead with every chance of losing it for the SDP, whereat, it was predicted, the new party would disintegrate. Here again, the predictions couldn't have been more predictable, especially from Tony Benn, who had branded the SDP a media party, with no policies. My own view was that for the SDP not to have the Labour Party's policies was policy enough, but a win for Jenkins still looked like a lot to hope for. Mark Thatcher got lost in Africa, which had to happen. The railway union ASLEF went on strike, which also had to happen. Freddie Laker's airline went broke, which seemed as if it had to happen too, since few realized at the time that an independent entrepreneur who complained about being sabotaged by BA might just have a case. In Northern Ireland, John de Lorean's factory for building gull-winged sports cars had proved to be the most efficient way of combusting the British tax payer's money since the ground-nut scheme.

Mrs Thatcher gained fewer points for denying funds to these crashed buccaneers than she lost for having presided over the new spirit of free enterprise in which they had somehow contrived to fail. Her principles were working against her. Michel Foot hailed the Peace of Bishop's Stortford, a new deal by which the Labour Party would somehow bind up the differences within itself, thus rendering the SDP superfluous. Abetting this process with unsurprisingly miraculous timing, a plot was uncovered: Labour's Militant Tendency had not only been conspiring to remove all non-Marxist MPs after the next election victory, they had written their plan down. Happening to meet Neil Kinnock and his charming family taking a half-term tour of St Paul's, I found him delighted by this development and was thus able to

114

get some personal colour into my poem, but things were looking pretty staid. At just this point my chosen year started behaving as if the power had been switched on.

Jenkins won in Hillhead. Overnight, like Eurydice glanced at by Orpheus on their way out of Hades, the Labour Party went backwards into history. There would be a new party of opposition. Mrs Thatcher would be hard pressed to defeat it. She was the most unpopular Prime Minister since, since . . . But just when we were absorbing the shock of these wonders, wonders were succeeded by epiphanies. Argentina occupied the Falklands. Lord Carrington – observing the quaint, not yet quite extinct custom by which Ministers who presided over catastrophes resigned in contrition – presented his embarrassed Prime Minister with his head, which for a while looked like the only thing she had to throw at General Galtieri. In the House of Commons nobody shouted louder for war than Michael Foot, but by left-wing intellectuals it was taken for granted that for Britain to fight would be a preposterous exercise in post-Imperial nostalgia, jingoism after the fact. One of my most brilliant friends published an article instructing the fleet to turn back.

The sinking of the *Belgrano* confirmed thinkers on the Labour Party's left-wing in all their suspicions about Mrs Thatcher. Actually, we can now see, those same thinkers were helping to sink the Labour Party, because nothing weakened the opposition to Mrs Thatcher like reluctance to admit that in the matter of the Falklands war she was a realist. The *Belgrano* had been a victim, not of her ruthlessness, but of the Royal Navy's long memory for the day when they let the *Bismarck* out of their sight, thereby almost losing a whole convoy and World War II along with it. The Falklands war, small-scale in historic terms, was still a momentous event, and Mrs Thatcher managed it well. The best way to counter her afterwards would have been to say, truthfully, that while to show determination in war is admirable, it is not as taxing as to show creative imagination in peace, when there is no single object in view. But nobody – at least nobody in the House of Commons – said so, and she came out of the war doubled in stature, with the Labour Party nowhere in sight, although as yet it would have taken a clairvoyant to spot that no other party or group of parties would have a chance against her either. With a glittering future seemingly assured, the SDP's choice of Dr Owen as its leader seemed merely stage-struck, not disastrous.

At Buckingham Palace, the Queen played host to an undistinguished visitor, one Fagan, who appeared beside her bed at dead of night to bum a cigarette. Suspicions that the Palace might not be quite so suavely in charge of its affairs as had been thought were soon quelled. The IRA bombed a military band in London: things were getting back to normal. In Cambridge an undergraduate poetess called Sue had a devastating effect on previously imperturbable dons, allegedly because of her fluent gift for the sonnet form, and not because of her beauty: things were very normal. History had left Britain and was happening out there in the world, as was only proper. Squeezed by Begin's invading armies, Yasser Arafat and the PLO pulled out of Beirut, whose ruins filled the world's television screens, except for the sad hiatus in which Princess Grace died – by accident, scarcely history at all, just terribly regrettable, a containable tragedy. Then it was the Lebanon again, where Begin and Sharon were responsible for an uncontainable tragedy – the massacre in the camps. All of us who believed in the state of Israel's right to exist had suddenly to face the fact that it was run by men too stupid to appreciate why getting stuck with a label like *massacre in the camps* was contra-indicated, PR-wise.

At the time, that was my pick for the incident that would have the most fatal resonance in the future. As things turned out, it just blended into a dreadful, seesawing sequence of atrocities which can probably never be ended; only, at best, brought to some kind of balance. A better choice for an event with a long shadow would have been the Royal decision to deny Koo Stark her manifest destiny as the bride of Prince Andrew. Discreet, strong-willed, keen for the job, as bright as any woman willing to share her life with the future Duke of York was ever going to be, Koo, though she had admittedly been photographed with her clothes off, at least looked good that way. Though we didn't yet know it, to shut her out left the way open for Sarah Ferguson, whose impact on Buckingham Palace would be roughly the same as that of alcohol on the Eskimos.

But to spot that would have taken a crystal ball. There were bigger issues where all the trends were already running but you just couldn't believe they would go on that way. My brilliant friend who had instructed the fleet to turn back gave up writing about British politics. Another brilliant friend still wrote about British politics but now did it from America. With Reagan and Thatcher triumphant, everything was blamed on their unscrupulous populism. No other reason than public gullibility could be adduced for their success. It had not yet become fully clear that the real reason for the success of the right was the collapse of the left. Throughout the West, the dream of the socialist state was already well embarked on its long day's dying, but you had to be a cynic to believe it.

In the East you had to be a fanatic to believe anything else, and the really big news of the year was precisely that – they were running out of fanatics. The most tremendous event of the year was the one that didn't happen. Lech Walesa wasn't rubbed out. Jaruzelski locked him up but didn't kill him. Brezhnev checked out, Andropov checked in, and still the Russians let the Poles get away with it. In December, Walesa walked free. The Soviet tanks didn't come. The will to rule by terror was gone. With that gone, the whole thing was doomed. Looking back from now, it is easy to see how everything followed from that one non-event. Looking forward from then, we didn't dare even guess.

EDMUND WHITE

1983

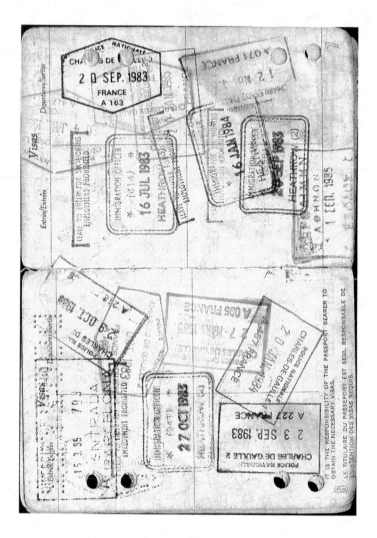

Stamps of Desire–
From Edmund White's passport

IN THE SUMMER of 1983 I moved to Europe – for just a year, I thought, but now ten years later I find myself still in Paris.

I'd received a Guggenheim fellowship, which allowed me to live anywhere I liked for a year, and I chose Paris because I'd always been intimidated by it. London was too much like New York in boring ways (dirty, pushy, expensive) and dissimilar in disturbing ways (snobbish, insular). I'd already lived for a year in Rome and for thirteen summers in Venice. Paris was all new and supremely civilized (safe streets, good food, hushed voices, more book stores than in all the United States) and sufficiently different from New York to be intriguing (non-confiding, very formal, hard to woo). Whereas a New York friendship must be transfused three times a day by whispered telephone calls, in Paris the cycle of renewal in a friendship is slower and much more decorous.

People ascribed my move to motives either above or below me, certainly to one side. Since I'd just published *A Boy's Own Story*, one New York editor said, 'You're just beginning to be well known here and you're getting out because you know you'll never write another successful novel if you stay here.' In fact, my very minor fame didn't distract me. Fame of any sort may bring out a real whorishness in Americans, but to

121

them literary fame is one of the least appealing and more dowdy forms of celebrity. In France I could enjoy the generic high status of being a writer without being a *known* writer. In France, there's a superstitious respect for writers in general, famous or obscure. A concierge in Paris has an automatic admiration for any dweller in her building who may be a writer; when I appeared on the legendary TV book chat show, *Apostrophes* (now defunct), my butcher also treated me with reverence for a whole week afterwards. In New York a janitor thinks a writer is a ne'er-do-well and can be convinced otherwise only be a no-nonsense read-out of sales figures and earnings. But in any event America is scarcely literate, the only country where a lawyer or doctor can tell you cheerfully, 'I don't read,' as though his or her confession were no more grave than saying, 'I don't bowl.'

If people in France are more interested in authors than in their work and review books more than they read them, nevertheless it was a novel (a novelistic) experience to meet men and women right out of Proust, who lived in the Faubourg St Germain, prided themselves on the number and quality of the writers around their table and felt they could gain points by pretending to have read the latest revisionist evaluation of Heidegger. Didn't someone once say hypocrisy is the homage vice pays to virtue? That it is also the morality of nations? In the United States no one feels even the need to *lie* about having read a book, a very bad sign, and those who do read are academics keeping up with colleagues ploughing the same field, or they are members of a ghetto (gay, black, feminist) confirming their own identity. No sense as there is in Paris that if one hasn't read this week's genius (or at least cobbled together a few opinions about him or her) one dare not dine out. And in America there is certainly no disinterested wallowing in a book for the pure pleasure of encountering a new sensibility or a turn of phrase. Everything in the States must serve a purpose – no wonder that even 'intellectuals' mostly read self-help books.

A few enemies said I'd moved to France to run away from all my friends dying of AIDS in New York. No one I knew, however, was actually dying as early as 1983; my heavy losses were to come. After 1985 each time I would fly back to New York it was to see a friend who'd lost another ten pounds, his hair, his lover, his mind, his life. One after another all but a few of my New York friends died and I became an expert in writing funeral orations. In 1983, however, this terrible toll was still waiting to be taken. I even wrote for *Vanity Fair* a cheerful essay about homosexual culture in which AIDS was dismissed as a temporary hitch soon to be eliminated in the triumphant march of gay liberation. So much for my writerly powers of divination as the antennae of the race.

At age forty-three I was enrolled in school again, this time at the Alliance française, and I spent hours every day looking up words. Just today I picked up my copy of Chateaubriand's *Memoirs* with all my marginal notes. Half of the words I translated I still don't know (*un polisson*, I see, is 'a scamp').

I was no longer a professor but a student, no longer someone whom people interviewed but an interviewer myself: I had a new job for American *Vogue* writing about the French cultural scene. I can remember my interview of Eric Rohmer, an austere, reclusive intellectual devoted to making films about silly suburban girls. I'd prepared my questions in French but I couldn't be sure of his answers. Luckily I taped them and made Gilles Barbedette, who was translating my books, decode Rohmer's remarks. Little did the poor editors of *Vogue* know how incompetent I was in my new language.

My linguistic inadequacy must have been all too apparent to the literary stars I was meeting at dinner parties – Hector Bianciotti, Philippe Sollers, Julia Kristeva, Michel Foucault, Pierre Guyotat. I learnt that the eyes always reveal incomprehension, so I picked up the habit of lowering my eyes modestly when people spoke to me. That new tic, plus my frequent blushes when I realized too late I'd said yes instead of no, gained me a reputation for being 'nice' (*gentil*), seldom a compliment in French.

No, I was learning a whole new set of attitudes – that left-wing politics, for instance, were definitely *démodé*. Whereas American intellectuals were still furious at Susan Sontag for having said two years earlier that communism is fascism with a human face, their French counterparts would have wearily agreed to everything except the mollifying 'with a human face'. After the Socialist triumph in 1981, French intellectuals no longer took an interest in politics, the paradoxical effect of gaining a victory.

If the French were becoming less political, they were also becoming more cosmopolitan. When I'd first visited France in the sixties I'd been struck by how chauvinistic and self-absorbed French culture had been. At a time when a dull levelling was making all Western countries resemble one another, France remained unique – different smells, clothes, ideas, gestures, passions. Barthes, Lacan, Lévi-Strauss – the French revered their thinkers (already a peculiar habit) and their thoughts, which were in no way commensurate with those being hatched in England and America, although the thoughts would eventually change the course of English-speaking linguistics and social philosophy.

By 1983, however, the peculiarly French way of doing things was losing steam at a time when the country was opening up to the outside world. Nearly a quarter of all French books published each year were translations (compared to less than 10 per cent in England, for instance). The French were reading the Japanese novels of Tanizaki, the thick experimental fiction of the 1920s by the Viennese master Von Doderer, the slim novellos of such contemporary Italians as Tabucchi and

Giudice, as well as the entertaining novels of David Lodge and Alison Lurie.

Of course all of these French enthusiasms (for foreign writers) and aversions (for progressive politics) were governed by modishness. In the English-speaking world ideas change in a slower, more haphazard way and intellectuals fear more betraying their principles than falling out of step. Even the phrase 'intellectual fashion' is a reproach in English, whereas being 'à la page' is a self-apparent virtue in French. In the United States ideas are held mostly by academics and each generation of structuralists or post-structuralists or semiologists terrorizes its elders with a new armamentarium of terms and concepts, but once the newcomers attain tenure their creed becomes enshrined (embalmed, some might say). America is the attic for storing in camphor outworn European ideas. Moreover, in the States ideas are long-lived. Feminists, for instance, are far more powerful now than they were twenty years ago; departments of women's studies (or gay studies, or African-American studies) exert a sometimes totalitarian influence over American intellectual life, wielding the right of virtual censorship. These tendencies were already discernible in 1983.

In France, however, things are organized completely differently. The 'politics of identity', so vital and successful in the States, are strenuously rejected in France – as a loss of human rights, of all things. Whereas Americans think only of special interest groups, lobbies, ethnic entities and local communities, the French are centrists who condemn American-style politics as 'marginalization'. Even in cultural life French centrism has an effect. In France there is no Jewish novel, no black novel, no gay novel; Jews, blacks and gays, of course, write about their lives, but they would be offended if they were discussed with regard to their religion, ethnicity or gender. When I was interviewed in 1983 by the French gay literary journal, *Masques* (now defunct), I was the first writer they'd ever queried who had responded yes to the question, 'Are you a gay writer?' When the first European gay literary conference was organized in London soon afterwards, France was the only country that sent but one representative, Geneviève Pastre; all the other French writers invited had indignantly refused because they despised the implied marginalization of the label.

In 1983 I saw such reactions as closetedness. From my American perspective the French seemed incapable of acknowledging their sexual identity. Now, ten years later, I have become sufficiently Gallicized that I see all these questions through cross-cultural bifocals. Americans now strike me as too forward in private life and too contentious in public life. The constant Balkanization into ever smaller political entities precludes any hope of domestic consensus (and a nearly complete indifference to public safety and international policy). Culturally, however, identity politics is rich and messy both in England and America. Michael Ondaatje, Toni

Morrison, Timothy Mo, Kazno Ishiguro, Armistead Maupin, Louise Erdrich, Derek Walcott, Salman Rushdie – this is a very partial list of the living treasures of our language. In France there is no comparable list of exotic and talented writers, although in recent years major literary prizes have gone to the Caribbean writer Patrick Chamoiseau, the Moroccan Tahar Ben Jalloun and the Argentine Hector Bianciotti.

Because I moved to France in 1983 I now have the courage to defy the deadening exigencies of American political correctness without fearing I am becoming a Republican. Because I moved to France in 1983 I see no conflict between an interest in fashion and high art or between a love of luxury and a commitment to progressive politics. Because I moved to France in 1983 I seek in my own writing to find the universal aspects of gay experience – and I have the freedom to write about even heterosexuality.

I am also, as a result, often guilty of what the French call *mauvaise foi*. When Stendhal met Byron at Parma he complained that Byron insisted the poets treat him as a noble and the nobles as a poet. I am capable of playing the American in Paris and the Parisian in New York, excoriating both my French friends for their modishness and my American friends for being out of fashion. As a sort of international gypsy I have learnt that in England one must be plain-spoken and ironic at one's own expense, in America one can be baroque but one must be self-assertive and in France one should rise above the mere anecdotic details of one's own life to the empyrean of general truth and if one is ironic it should be at someone else's expense. If moving has cut me off from the evolving American social reality (if not from my American memories) it's also given me the knack of seeing double, so useful to the novelist, so disturbing to the individual.

MARK LAWSON

1984

Pope in Ugandan Discussions

THE USUAL WAY in which history works is that the dates of destiny – the years which, when mentioned, trigger a list of swift significances – are established only in retrospect. Merely say now the digits of 1914, 1936, 1945, 1963, 1966 and, as with a numerical code on a briefcase or safe, there is a click and a sheaf of pictures spills out: bloodstained khaki, a limousine in Dallas, a huddle of red shirts round a gold cup.

But there are just a few dates which, more like a burglar alarm, ring bells as you approach them. They are the booby-trapped years. Millenia are one example. For us, 2000 begins to bleep menacingly already as we come within reach of its beam. And 1984 was the other one, a code programmed in advance against contemporary trespassers, though this time rigged by literature rather than history.

In fact, I'd been told by my English teacher that Orwell's title *Nineteen Eighty-Four* was a reversal of the date in which he was writing, a time loosely in the future, rather than a chronological prediction, a bet on a historical horse. I can remember now my English teacher saying – this would have been 1976, the year in which we studied the Orwell, as third-formers – 'When 1984 comes around, people will go through this book, saying, yah-boo, George, you got it wrong. But they would be very, very stupid to do this.'

Despite my teacher's strictures, people, or at least journalists, did indeed spend 1984 doing exactly that very, very stupid thing, all over the national press. And I suppose that third-formers given *Nineteen Eighty-Four* to study today struggle with its peculiar double-remove, a book of the past whose future is also apparently behind them. But I find it difficult, from my current perspective, to be too hard on the press for hanging themselves on such a tempting peg. For them, it must have been the calendar equivalent of a Canon Chasuble becoming Archbishop of Canterbury. (Although, now I think of it, only the *Independent* and the *Guardian* have ever mentioned Henry Fielding in reviews of the singer Tom Jones.)

It is also the case that, when I tap the four-digit combination 1–9–8–4 into my head, without consulting any reference books first, the main pictures offered actually are terribly Orwellian: the ranks of riot-shielded police at Orgreave, some of them, in fact, soldiers, according to persistent left-wing conspiracy theory. The illustrations provided by the 1984 miners' strike of the ways in which a state operated – of how the press and the police could be employed as instruments of it – did seem like a small joke played by fate with the date. Orwell's shade must also have enjoyed his title-date taking in the election of Ronald Reagan for a second term, which I can work out without research must have happened in that year because of the quadrennial pattern of presidential elections. The only other response I get from 1–9–8–4 tapped in cold is that there must have been an Olympics in that year, and that I suspect it was the one in which Sebastian Coe won gold.

And, having allowed myself a flick through *Chronicle of the 20th Century* between this sentence and the last, I can confirm that Sebastian Coe did lift the yellow medal in the men's 1500 metres. But I had forgotten that 1984 was the year in which the IRA nearly blew up Margaret Thatcher and her Cabinet at Brighton. I also discover that, during what looks like a rough twelve months for politicians, Mrs Gandhi was shot, General Secretary Andropov's kidneys failed him, Prime Minister Pierre Trudeau resigned, and that a former Nigerian transport minister was discovered drugged and bound in a crate at Stansted airport. The AIDS virus was isolated – a vaccine was promised by doctors within two years – and James Fixx, the great guru of American joggers, died of a heart attack while jogging in Vermont.

I had forgotten that some of these events took place at all, nudged others into earlier or later years. It is, I suppose, because of the tendency of events to coalesce or simply to dissolve that 'Name The Year' events are such a staple of radio shows. But I also have that excuse for amnesia or confusion which we can all use: that the 1984 in *Chronicle of the 20th Century* was not my 1984. Although only some dates set off the historical alarm, all years are personally booby-trapped. Tapping in the code 1–9–8–4 to the file marked 'Personal' rather than 'World', I get, inevitably, not a small spool of newsreel but a feature film, a movie starring me.

The film is called *Ruler of the Universe*. Its hero, or at least central character, is a twenty-two-year-old. Its setting is summer. Its plot is loss of innocence. In the opening scene, the boy meets a middle-aged man on a train.

It was May 1984. The train was running on what was known to commuters as the Bed-Pan line, a disgruntled construction from the line's terminating (generally late-terminating) stations of Bedford and St Pancras, but possibly also a reference to the stained and squalid tin receptacles which made up the trains. I was heading for Harpenden, a Hertfordshire village swelled by the immigration of rich London businessmen who didn't want to live in their workplace. A more exotic resident, the comedian Eric Morecambe, would occasionally shout 'Harpenden!' as an expression of surprise or pain in sketches on the *Morecambe and Wise* television show. I had grown up in Harpenden – with the usual adolescent yells of surprise and pain – and was going back there, on that day, to visit my parents.

In my memory's rent-out video of this moment, I am reading one of the six daily newspapers I purchased. I'd had this bad paper habit since the age of about ten. My father – though a businessman, not a journalist –

came home each evening with a soft-leather briefcase pregnant with the British press. In my adolescence, my mother briefly introduced a rule that I must engage him in conversation for a few minutes before making a lunge for the wedge of newsprint. All of this was part of my desperate ambition to become a journalist. But I could not, on that May day on the train, have been much further away from fulfilling it.

Through the ink and paper barrier, the man opposite said my name. I knew of him better than I knew him. My mother had taught his children at the local Catholic school. He was called Gerry McGuinness. He asked what I was doing now. I said that I worked for a publishing company in the advertising department. This was the form of words I had agreed with myself for enquiries about my occupation. In fact, I was selling advertising space for an accountancy magazine.

At the time, the media pages of the *Guardian* – which the ambitious scanned like the superstitious read horoscopes – consisted mainly of advertisements pretending not to involve 'selling space', as it was known. In turn, those liberal humanities students who got the jobs would pretend that that was not what they were doing.

This was partly a middle-class snobbery about the selling professions, although those who become journalists soon acknowledge, if they are sensible, that their wages are paid by the advertising department. But it was also, in my case, that I was seriously temperamentally unsuited to the task. The selling system we operated was called A–I–D–A which did not, as you might think, involve singing at the businessmen until they gave in. A–I–D–A was an acronym. I remember that the I was for Interest, the D was for Desire and the last A designated Acceptance but the significance of the first A now escapes me. Perhaps it was for Answer the telephone, except that, as I shiveringly recall, the point was that you had to ring these people up: 'cold calling'.

But Desire, anyway, was the most important element. In fact, the approach to marketing was insistently sub-erotic. 'Shall I put it in again, Mr Jones?' Sloanes would croon into the phone, referring to an advertisement already run the previous week. If a businessman was frighteningly crusty, we were told to imagine him sitting on the lavatory. This was supposed to demystify him. In fact, given that you had never met the (usually) man at the other end of the line, I found this trick difficult. When I tried it, I received a bizarre image of a faceless, weightless pinstripe crouched above the pan, like Claude Rains having a crap in some suppressed out-take of *The Invisible Man*. The approach, anyway, rarely helped me to move him along from Interest to Desire.

On the train, Mr McGuinness asked, rather shrewdly, whether I was happy working for a publishing company in the advertising department. I said that I wanted to be a journalist but that it was almost impossible to get into nowadays, unless you knew someone or you had gone to Oxford or Cambridge. (I was London.) In reply, he handed me a white business card. It said: Managing Director of The Universe.

Looking back, this has always seemed to me like a scene from one of those winsome American movies in which the deity comes to modern New York in the shape of an ageing film star. 'Who are you?' gasps the beleaguered hero, helped by this kindly stranger on the subway. 'Listen, son, let's just say I'm the Managing Director of The Universe, OK?' replies the stranger, winking.

In fact, in this case, Mr McGuinness was not God, as such, but rather part of His public relations effort on Earth. *The Universe* was a weekly Catholic newspaper, Mr McGuinness was the managing director. He suggested that I might like to come and work there for three months in the summer. Not much money, he cautioned, but I could see how I liked things. Think about it and phone him. Two days later, I accepted.

The Universe seemed, as it still does, a splendidly impressive name for a newspaper. I discovered early on the thrill of picking up the telephone in the office and saying, 'The Universe.' Doing so always reminded me of Professor Welch's 'History speaking!' in *Lucky Jim*.

As Catholic newspapers go, *The Universe* was probably unusual in that the star columnist was a Jewish rabbi and the associate editor a former Hollywood movie star who had appeared opposite Vivien Leigh.

139

The former was Rabbi Lionel Blue, who had begun, as the newspaper's cookery columnist, the curious fusion of theology and recipes which was to make him a media star. The latter was Keiron Moore, who had appeared in Korda's 1947 version of *Anna Karenina*, with Vivien Leigh and Ralph Richardson.

Keiron subsequently appeared in a large number of other films, including *The League of Gentlemen* and *Day of the Triffids*, before abandoning acting to work for a Catholic charity. He had then moved into Catholic journalism.

It was a strange career plan. This was the time of Ronald Reagan's presidency and I remember thinking once, as Keiron worked on an editorial about US policy in Latin America, that there was probably not another newspaper in the world in which the commentator on Reagan was himself a former movie star. Keiron was a helpful colleague and has remained a friend, but he could be demanding to his staff. One of the sub-editors, after a long day of being subject to the old actor's perfectionism, would go home and watch over and over again the moment in *Day of the Triffids* when Keiron was devoured by a plant. Can there ever have been an equivalent circumstance in journalism, of the staff having access to such satisfying therapy?

I had assumed before arrival that assignments at *The Universe* would be mainly church fêtes and singing nuns, but, in fact, the trick was to find a Roman twist to the main stories of the day. This is the case with all specialist publications. The *Irish Times* is famously supposed to have carried, during a rail strike, the front page story: 'Thousands of commuters – many of them Irish – struggled to work today.' In the same way, we would scan death lists of major disasters for Marys and Josephs and O'Connors and Learys who might provide us with an angle. Somewhere else in London, the staff of a computer magazine were probably sweating over the same lists for a deceased programmer to fill their space.

My next piece of luck was that *The Universe* was so small that there could be no reporters' hierarchy. Indeed, the first piece I ever wrote was carried on the front page. THEOLOGIAN JOINS ROW OVER FROZEN EMBRYOS was the headline, the byline was EXCLUSIVE BY MARK LAWSON, and the piece began: 'A Catholic theologian in Australia has entered the debate on the future of two frozen embryos . . .'

There is a newspaper saying that the only true 'exclusive' is a story no one else would want, and I suppose that this applies to my embryo piece, but I was and am devoutly proud of it. I vaguely recall having stayed in the office until midnight, chasing the Australian theologian by telephone around the state of Victoria, and then having caught the milk-train home before getting up at dawn to come back in and write the story. In retrospect, this kind of behaviour looks uncomfortably like crazed ambition, and I cannot swear it wasn't, but I remember it as a terror of being sacked from that one job.

Not all of the early stories, however, were as exciting as the frozen Aussie embryos. 'Cardinal Hume is expected to attend, as are celebrity Catholics Eamonn Andrews and Derek Nimmo,' begins one article – not this time, apparently, an exclusive – about a church fête to raise funds for the rebuilding of a graveyard wall.

Nor were all the assignments successful. One Friday afternoon, I was despatched to a block of flats in Peckham, where the Blessed Virgin Mary was said to have appeared to an elderly resident and warned her that she had left the gas on. Regrettably, when I arrived, the recipient of the vision had gone out shopping. The press office of the local gas board said they would ring back with a comment, but never did.

Uneasy with such piety, the younger staff – who included John Walsh, an Irish sub-editor with a Wildean drawl and brave waistcoats, who seemed worryingly to be as ambitious as I was – sometimes privately livened up the paper. Sub-editing a piece on the foreign pages about the Pope's meeting with a bishop from a particular part of Africa, we gleeful young fans of *Private Eye* affixed the headline: POPE IN UGANDAN DISCUSSIONS.

Two weeks into my summer attachment, the editor – a sparky woman of Lithuanian Catholic descent called Rowanne Pasco – asked to see me. She said that Dan, who wrote the paper's television preview column, was keen to retire. Dan had a bad leg and, therefore, had not gone to see the programmes before writing about them.

My legs, on the other hand, said Rowanne, looked reasonably sound and, if I wanted to see the stuff before writing about it, there were things called previews I could attend. It was another piece of luck.

And that was how, in the summer of 1984, I discovered Room B309 at BBC television centre. It was a windowless basement bunker in which, each Friday, all of those who wrote advance notices of television programmes for newspapers sat with a stack of sandwiches and watched perhaps eight or ten consecutive cassettes. On my first Friday, one of the older critics barked, after a fancy camera movement in a drama, 'Oh my God, I think it's going to be imaginative!' Later, when I tentatively reached for an egg sandwich, another of the senior previewers snapped: 'Leave the salmon for the regulars.'

On my third Friday, a man called Peter Davalle, who wrote for *The Times*, said that he was going on holiday, had just lost his regular replacement, and would I send him a couple of my cuttings. I sent him the only two columns I had so far written for *The Universe*, saying that these were my most recent pieces, a claim which *The Universe*'s agony uncle, Father Paul, would have thought 'Jesuitical'.

One Thursday afternoon, when I was half-way through a story about a Catholic Church report on the moral effects of television soap opera, Peter Davalle rang and invited me to deputize for two weeks.

'Well, bloody hell, it could make you believe there's a God,' said one of *The Universe* sub-editors when I told him.

On the first three days of my stint, *The Times* printers went on strike and I began to fear that God wanted me to stay at *The Universe*. But, soon, I was spending as much time working for other papers as for my employer. I cultivated a trick, when I needed to be elsewhere, of leaving a jacket draped over the back of my chair.

'He can't be far away. His jacket's here,' my colleagues would tell the editors. When *The Universe* relocated to Manchester in the late eighties, I had a phone call asking me if I would like to reclaim a jacket of mine which had been found during the London clean-out.

So that was my 1984. It was all so weird that it would not have bloody surprised me for one moment if the clocks *had* started striking thirteen.

Time's whirligig often seems like time's whirligiggle. Two years a journalist, I was offered a job on the arts pages of the *Independent*, a new daily newspaper. I employed the flamboyant ex-*Universe* sub-editor, John Walsh, as a television critic and, in 1993, he became my editor at the *Independent Magazine*, thus proving that God's journalistic workers really did move in mysterious ways.

In 1991, Picador published my first book, *Bloody Margaret: Three Political Fantasies*. In the opening novella, the hero is employed by a specialist dental magazine with offices near Farringdon, which some of my former *Universe* colleagues claimed to find familiar. There is a scene in which the hero trawls through the listed victims of a train crash, trying to find a dentist who will give him the front-page splash he is seeking.

And at each step of my career – to me, a series of wonderfully lucky chances, to others the result of dementedly ambitious calculation – I have always remembered that summer. The summer when I met a man on a train and lost my innocence, the summer when I became a journalist.

TAMA JANOWITZ

1985

Tama and Andy

ALL YEAR WE HAD what we called 'The Blind Date Club'. The core group consisted of me, Paige Powell and Andy Warhol. Every week Andy took us to a different restaurant. Each of us was responsible for finding a date for someone else. It began like this: my cousin Jeff Slonim worked at *Interview* magazine. One day he called up and said, 'Paige Powell has asked me to call you and see if you are free to come to dinner tonight with her and a blind date she's supposed to meet.'

I scarcely knew Paige Powell, the advertising director of *Interview*. I had seen her in various nightclubs, wearing extraordinary costumes, surrounded by photographers. She was one of those people who always seemed to be in a spotlight, even when on closer inspection it turned out there were no spotlights around. She generated her own intense radiation. I thought it was very nice of her to include me on her blind date, especially since I barely knew her. 'But why would she do this, Jeff?' I said. My cousin didn't know.

'She's just being friendly, I think,' he said. A little while later he called back. He said that Paige had now invited *him* to come on the blind date. 'Great!' I said. Then the phone rang again. It was Jeff. Andy Warhol, who owned *Interview* and was a good friend of Paige's, heard Jeff telling me about the blind date and decided to come along.

149

It was now me, Paige, Jeff, Andy Warhol and the blind date, all meeting up at the Odeon at 9.00, but Paige had neglected to inform the blind date that the date no longer consisted of just the two of them.

We all arrived at approximately the same time. Andy brought five men with him. The blind date was not at all surprised. He seemed to think it was entirely ordinary. We sat at a big round table, the blind date positioned in between me and Paige. To either side sat Andy, the five men and my cousin Jeff.

The blind date appeared to have been sent from Central Casting. He was very short, balding, wearing a gold chain, gold rings and a Hawaiian print shirt unbuttoned to his navel. He had a hairy chest, too. Though Paige and I didn't know each other very well, we worked together quite naturally as a team. First the blind date lectured Paige for ten minutes, and then Paige would flash me a warning and I would distract him and let him bore me for ten minutes. Andy watched this with fascination.

After that night he decided he wanted to do it every week. But each of us should have a date. He didn't want us to call it a Blind Date Dinner, though – he wanted to call them advertising or business dinners. I guess this meant it could be a tax write-off. Plus, I think he found it humiliating to be thought of as a guy who had to be fixed up on a date.

We went to Mr Chow's, Le Cirque, Le Bernadin, The Ritz Café, Odeon, Café Luxembourg, S.O.B.'s,

Texarkana and dozens of other restaurants. Andy always paid. I was living in a one-room apartment at that time. One day I measured my living quarters. It was ten feet by thirteen feet. I had practically never even eaten in a restaurant before. My clothes came from thrift stores. When it got cold Andy and Paige bought me a winter coat.

It was bizarre to go from one extreme to the other. Among my dates were film directors, an Italian count, a stockbroker, a journalist, artists, a gossip columnist, an anthropologist – dozens upon dozens of men. I can scarcely now remember any of them. One after the next fell in love with Paige.

The tension level of the evenings was extremely high. If one of the invited guests wasn't nervous about being out on a blind date, then he was nervous about being at a dinner with Andy Warhol. Once, early on, while making a reservation, Paige let it slip that the event was a group blind date – with Andy Warhol. That night our table was surrounded by a vast group of giggling, snickering waiters and busboys – six or seven at all times, peering and winking at us. After that we tried not to mention just what it was we were doing.

After a short time we ran out of single people we knew who were appropriate to invite. Then we included another man, known amongst ourselves as The Procurer.

He had to provide dates for the three of us, and sometimes himself as well. He had to take us all out to dinner; his driver, in a huge, ancient Daimler, picked us up and took us home. That meant, when he was invited, that there were eight of us on the blind date. We could almost never find a date for The Procurer, but this didn't bother him: he had friends at a modelling agency, and they would send along any new girl in town. Occasionally we let one or two other men participate in this fashion instead of him.

Sometimes we had a giant group blind date. One night we had twenty people on the date – ten friends, and ten strangers. Everyone had to procure for someone else. The friends sat on one side and the dates were seated opposite. Unfortunately that was the night we picked a restaurant with live music and nobody could hear a single thing. Some of the people had not been informed as to what the purpose of the dinner was, and they seemed particularly baffled.

After dinner we usually went to a nightclub, dumping our dates or, less often, allowing them to come along. It was fun going to a nightclub with Andy. The crowd at the door magically parted, we were ushered in and once inside a sort of electrical charge would flicker through the air. 'Andy's here. Andy's here.' Immediately the whole energy level of the place went up, everyone seemed to feel they could now safely assume they were in the right spot – it had just received the most fashionable seal of approval.

I also enjoyed watching Andy out in public. He went out because he genuinely enjoyed it. It was obvious he wouldn't have kept going out, night after night, for thirty years, unless he really liked doing it. Some people said he went out so much for business purposes, but believe me there was no business to be found in those nightclubs. He liked seeing the latest places, and especially young kids. At the time I thought, gosh, doesn't he ever want to stay home? In a way I suppose it was like a drug, having that much attention paid to him. People came up to him constantly. They said things like, 'Oh, Andy, my cousin met you fifteen years ago, you know her – Judy Smockowski?' Andy always smiled graciously and asked them some questions. Then, suddenly, after a few minutes, came the cut-off point. It was exactly like a curtain falling. He wasn't rude, but this invisible curtain just fell. Then the person who had been gibbering away about their cousin he had met once fifteen years ago for two minutes at some book-signing, would suddenly look embarrassed, stop talking and slink away. Andy never did anything rude, he was always friendly, but then this cut-off point came, his eyes went blank, and the person got the message that the audience was over.

He liked mostly to talk about peculiar diseases and psychic phenomena and by sheer chance one time I fixed him up with a nice Jewish doctor and he was more excited about that date than anyone else who had ever come on the dates before. Unfortunately the doctor already had a boyfriend, and it was really sad because I couldn't tell Andy that the reason this doctor wasn't interested in him was because he lived with someone.

The rule was, on the blind dates, the date had to be single, not married or living with someone. But I was desperate to find Andy a date, and so I just called whoever I could think of, since I never thought Andy would actually want to see the person again. And now I couldn't let him know the doctor wasn't single, or he would have been really mad.

One time I actually was dating someone and I got my date to come and pick me up at 11.30, after the group blind date, and Andy later said to Paige, in a peevish voice, that I was breaking the rules by having another date on the same night.

And both Paige and I knew how angry he would have been if he had found out what we sometimes did: we ran out of people to invite, and The Procurer ran out of people to invite, and we had to come up with a date. Basically we began to call up friends of friends of friends of friends, who were in actuality complete strangers, and then we had to say, 'Listen, I know you don't know me – I'm sort of a friend of so-and-so's, who, actually, I guess you don't really know either – but I was wondering, could you come out on a blind date with me, another person and Andy Warhol?'

One time a guy agreed but decided not to come, and sent another guy instead. Since I had never met him, but couldn't let Andy know this, I had to pretend I knew him. It was only later I found out this stranger wasn't a stranger named Dan (which is what I kept calling him) but a stranger named Archie. I suppose it didn't really matter though.

Another time the date cancelled a half-hour before dinner, and I ended up knocking on the door of two men who lived down the hall from me. I had only chatted with them, walking our dogs, very briefly before this. But now I said, 'I know I don't know you very well. But could one of you just please drop whatever you're doing and come to dinner on a blind date with Andy Warhol – in, say, *the next ten minutes?*'

At the same time Paige was frantically scrambling to come up with someone, too. The guys who lived on my floor looked perplexed, and frightened. They decided against it. So I got on the phone, fast.

By some miracle, each of us got a guy to show up at the restaurant. Each thought he was Andy's date. Andy was alarmed. He was seated between *two* men. He didn't have the slightest idea which was supposed to be his date. Probably he thought one or the other of them was my date. Or Paige's. Anyway, he knew there was someone extra at this dinner. The rule was, one date per person – and he was a stickler for rules. So he completely ignored one guy. He just refused to speak to him. The person I had come up with was very clever. When he came in the restaurant he came to our table. 'Hi, Tama!' he said, turning his head fast. That way he could fake the fact that he really had no idea who I was. We had to pretend we were old friends: there was no way Andy would have tolerated the humiliation of having a complete stranger at our meal.

But the remarkable thing was, that this man, a complete unknown, looked exactly like a younger version of Andy. People all over the restaurant were whispering, 'Is that his cousin? Is that his nephew?' He had white hair, pale skin, and glasses that were just like Andy's. It was uncanny. And to make matters better, he was also a doctor – a nutritionist. Food and vitamins and any sort of cosmetics was another favourite topic for Andy.

It was only the second time that Andy showed a genuine interest in his date. But when he asked him out again, the doctor showed up – with a date. This made Andy furious. His feelings were deeply hurt.

Not a single blind date ever worked out or led to anything else – not even a second date. And we did this once or twice a week for two years.

On New Year's Eve, 1986, we didn't have our blind date but a friend took us all to dinner at the River Café. I saw recently in the paper that this restaurant, on New Year's Eve, has a special rate of $325 per person. I have never done such glamorous things before nor since. It was just us and a few friends. Afterwards Paige, Andy and me took one of the man's cars-with-driver – the man and the others stayed on – and headed back into Manhattan. As we crossed the Brooklyn Bridge fireworks began to explode all around us, overhead. It was exactly midnight. On the radio the Rolling Stones began to play '19th Nervous Breakdown', and the three of us began singing along and laughing. I don't know why, it was just such a perfect moment, to be in this luxurious old car at midnight with the fireworks and the skyline of Manhattan before us.

Ever since that first blind date, Paige has been the most wonderful friend: trustworthy, supportive and generous. I feel lucky to know her, with her mysterious animal grace and unique imagination.

Andy loved her, too. He died less than two months after that New Year's Eve.

After his death, various people came to help settle his estate and help create the Warhol Foundation. One night Paige invited Tim Hunt, who had come from London to join a group of us for drinks. It was, I suppose a sort of blind date. A few years later we were married.

DAVID PROFUMO

1986

With Tom

THE YEAR OF 1986 was for me so full of psychodynamic turbulence that I am unlikely to forget it. A lot of stuff happened – the ladies of Liechtenstein finally got the vote, Iceland laid claim to Rockall, Madame Marcos showed the world several hundred clean pairs of heels: but what I remember best is that Helen and I were both pregnant, and had tricky deliveries. Also, I shared a room with a human corpse for the first time.

My year had a happy middle and end, but it started with an unique feat of publishing. For some while Graham Swift and I had been compiling an anthology about our shared passion, fishing (I don't see why people find this odd – was Yeats scoffed at when he took up fencing, or Kipling when he painted his balls red so he could continue to play golf in the snow? Well, then). By virtue of an extraordinary mix-up, Picador had published its paperback version of *The Magic Wheel* just before Christmas 1985, whereas the hardback edition appeared from Heinemann in the middle of January 1986. This is not a marketing strategy I am aware has been replicated anywhere else in the world, but it did kind of set the tone for my personal year, during which I was struggling to finish my first novel.

At the end of January, the US Space Shuttle *Challenger* exploded seventy-three seconds after lift-off from

Cape Canaveral, killing its seven astronauts. Apparently, NASA had ignored warnings from the manufacturers that cold weather might adversely affect the booster rockets. One of the dead was Christa McAuliffe, a school teacher from Concorde, New Hampshire: by coincidence, we were due to visit a friend who was also teaching in the same town, and even when we arrived (in April) the place was in deep mourning. The inhabitants were thunderstruck, dumbfounded. It was the first time I had witnessed the emotional aftermath of a disaster that had subsumed a heterodox community, at every level.

Later that year, the Singer company announced it was no longer going to be making sewing machines, but was diversifying into components for the aerospace industry.

On the morning of April 26th at the Chernobyl nuclear power station in the Ukraine 1000 megawatts reactor Number Four blew up, and the blaze took a fortnight to extinguish. It was certainly not the first disaster along these lines (there had been an explosion in the Mayak depot back in 1957) but the scale and circumstances of this made it one of the mythopoeic disasters of the second half of this century. Some 696,000 Soviet citizens were examined, and by the end of the year more than 37,000 had been sent to hospital. One estimate of those at risk from contamination puts the figure at 100,000 people – those exposed to doses of radiation greater than one hundred rems (then the unit of measurement) run the risk of blindness, leukaemia and thyroid cancers. The official death toll was thirty-one.

Huge tracts of the old USSR have been rendered desolate for centuries, but of course people continue to live there, despite the levels of caesium 134. The statistics about carcinomas and mutant foetuses only came to light earlier this year: 1986 was, you may remember, the year of 'openness', or Glasnost.

Just as the dust was – literally – settling on this nightmare I was on a brief trip north, and went to get another glimpse of the island of Gruinard, off the west coast of the Scottish Highlands. To me, it is one of the loneliest and most chilling places in Britain.

In the summer of 1942, the small military contingent there was joined by nine civilians armed with glass flasks. Thirty sheep were procured from the local crofters, and were transported over to the deserted island, which lies not far offshore. The animals were tethered, and a 25-pound bomb was exploded nearby. That night, the only sound from Gruinard was that of sheep coughing themselves to death: the bomb contained spores of anthrax, a zoonotic bacillary infection that is 90 per cent fatal when transmitted to humans, causing lung infections, paralysis and excruciating black swellings.

In 1943, the germ warfare weapon was 'improved' so that it could be dropped from a low-flying bomber. Later that year (despite the fact that a carcase had drifted ashore, and caused a minor outbreak of the disease on the mainland), munitions workers at Porton Down were busy packing millions of cattle cakes with these spores. The war ended before the Allies' plan to bomb six German cities was put into operation.

I was staring across at this sad island (still off-limits, and reputed to be populated with melanistic rabbits) for a reason. At the heart of the novel I was writing was a report in a Hebridean newspaper that a germ warfare experiment had been conducted off Lewis as late as 1953, when a raftload of monkeys had been sprayed with a virulent strain of pneumonia. One reader wrote in with a story that one of the carcases had been washed ashore. The MP for the Western Isles raised the matter in Parliament, and was told the information was classified for many years to come. I was standing there to remind myself of the secret that was the seed-crystal for my current fictional preoccupation, set in the Cold War years, but seamlessly connected to the present day.

Gloom was replaced by *joie de vivre* in June, when Helen gave birth to 8 pounds and 6 ounces of Tom, a brother for James. I am squeamish about all aspects of human parturition, and was relieved to learn that the birth was to be induced, so I slipped away from the delivery room for an hour to check that my copy had reached the *Sunday Times* safely (I was a regular reviewer for the literary pages in those days, when it was still a decent newspaper). Our second son was born, after a bit of a struggle by Mary the brilliant *accoucheuse*, shortly after my return. Once again, we experienced that pervasive sense of anxiety that you get when there is a small baby in your life: we took him home, and at once I reran my familiar, apocalyptic nightmares. Our sleeps were scuppered by feeds, our daylight hours shared with a precocious three-year-old (has anyone done a study of how prolonged exposure to a toddler can bugger up your command of English?), but, all things considered, we never forgot for one moment how lucky we were.

Helen had taken a little time off from her career as a television producer, but 1986 was the deadline year for me to finish my novel, *Sea Music*. I was doing a lot of freelance journalism – I reviewed over a hundred books that year, a personal endurance record I only broke in 1989, when, as a Booker judge, I managed to read 26,424 pages of fiction in three months – but the novel was the thing. It was going very slowly, but then, at the end of June, the engines of creativity just ground to a halt. For the first time in my life I came up against what Russell Hoban has dubbed 'Blighter's Rock'. I felt each day was a long walk down a derelict headland, lonely and misguided. I lost faith in my storyline, and found my characters as appealing as a Soviet picnic. In my small, hot, dark red study, with its stalagmite piles of other people's books rising everywhere from the carpet, I smoked so many cigarettes that the place looked like a nephelosphere. I stared so hard at my typewriter that beads of blood began to form on my forehead. Things were not looking too good.

I now know a little about the novelist's life. It boils down to: making things up, applied typing, artificially self-induced confidence, and luck. Then, I was learning the love-hate relationship an author has with words. The days squirmed by, and increasingly I came to resemble some Grub Street denizen – stubbly, papuliferous, spattered with Tipp-Ex, not quite sixteen annas to the rupee, slouching towards dementia and in danger (like Gérard de Nerval) of parading a pet lobster on a ribbon. My mental iatrohydraulic system was about to back up. As Dr Hunter S. Thompson put it: The Weasels Are Closing In.

Why was this happening to me? Two thoughts on that, but no fingers of blame attaching. Most writers go nuts when up against it – sponge-divers get nosebleeds and roofing contractors called Barry often contract 'buildersbum'. There was something wonky in my literary-cerebral plumbing, that was all, and as a result I suffered an airblock and much spectral rattling in the pipes before a thin gleet of rusty, precious prose began to appear in my desperate cup, later that summer.

A fiction editor at a leading London publisher had expressed an interest in my work-in-progress. There had been talk of a commission. On June 30th, I went to Fabers to hear his verdict about the first half of the book. He said he was disappointed by the way it had turned out, and felt it was not going to be one for them (a phrase, I think, that may be familiar to many writers).

For the record, it went on to be published by someone else, and in 1989 I was gratified to accept the Geoffrey Faber Memorial Prize from Lady Faber in the board-room of that very company. For me, it was a nice moment.

The second reason for my lack of progress was that I am a very superstitious writer, and I like to work in a limbo that denies clock-time by drawing down the blinds on my window, and neutralizing conditions by working only under my electric lights. A guest (that teacher from Concorde, as it happened) pulled up the blinds in my study, where he was sleeping, and that spooked me, stupidly, for several weeks.

At the end of September, one of my uncles died quite suddenly in his bed, of a cardiac arrest. My parents were abroad, so I was summoned to the scene. I was required to spend an unnerving part of that morning in a chair sitting alone opposite him, where his heart had exploded, until the authorities arrived. Police, and undertakers, and acquaintances, eventually traipsed through. But I have to say that 1986 was not a year that reinforced my confidence in the lukewarm notion one might have of Authorities, in general.

It had a happy ending, though, as I promised. The novel got finished, and I raised the blinds in my study. It was raining outside in the dark, but I was happy. I was also lucky: *Sea Music* became one of the 54,746 UK titles to be published two years later, and it is still in print.

I do not hold it against them, but the editorial gurus at Picador turned it down. Since then, they have seen the light. Happy Birthday anyway: excellent publishers are still far and few. My lobster agrees.

COLM TÓIBÍN

1987

The Art of Losing

In Barcelona

YOU LEFT BARCELONA at the end of that summer so you don't know what happened then. I know how bad your memory is but I think you might remember the last silent meal at the table in my flat in Carrer d'Avinyo, and the trip on the metro to the station, and how we embraced for as long as we could in front of all the people who were settling down for the long night's journey to Paris. I was embarrassed and wanted to get away.

I worked hard after you left. I had never been in love with anyone before and I presumed things ended easily. I kept you out of my mind as I finished my book. But when it got cold I wanted to go home. I contacted my newspaper in Dublin and I said that I would be back. I booked a ticket, and a few days before Christmas Evelyn helped me with all my luggage to a taxi on Carrer Princesa. I was vomiting and retching in the street in fear and knowledge that my time was up. Maybe I had a hangover as well, but I don't want to go into that just now.

On the plane I realized that I was going to London first and you were there too and it would be easy to contact you. I was frightened by the sudden knowledge that I desperately wanted to see you. It would be simple to telephone you; I still had your number in my head. Even your voice on your answer machine would be enough. But I could not face your real voice. Maybe I would catch a flight straight to Dublin. Maybe I would wait for a while in Heathrow, think about it. Maybe I would leave my options open. I don't know if you know this but I have always, no matter what, been able to calculate.

I made a decision: I knew that most flights to Dublin were booked up; if I could get a seat on a plane today I would go, and if not I would phone you. Let fate, or the volume of traffic across the Irish Sea, decide. There were free seats on every flight, they told me when I made my way from Terminal 2 to Terminal 1, and I booked a ticket for later that evening. I was relieved. I would not have to see you.

I rang Imogen Parker at Curtis Brown. She was my agent then. You will remember going to a party in her house. She thought that you were beautiful. I don't know if I ever told you that. And that day in her office in Regent Street she told me that she had a publisher for my novel, and I was frightened by this, as much as I would have been had I heard your voice. I said that everything was going to change now.

I still could have rung you. I could have changed my flight. Even on the tube I could have got off at Hammersmith or Hounslow or Hounslow East and found a telephone and asked you if it was OK if I came around. I am in London, I tried to imagine my own voice. But I did nothing. I met a journalist I knew in the bar in Heathrow and we had a few drinks and I flew home.

That night I sat on a stool at a high table in the airport bar with my luggage all around me. There was no point in phoning you now. I was here, and I waited until the bar closed before I caught a taxi home.

I had not paid the mortgage for at least six months and no telephone bill or electricity bill. I still had a key, but the building society could have come and changed the locks. I hadn't bothered to ask anyone to send on the post. I knew that it would just be bills, and I had no money to pay bills.

I left the luggage on the street and pushed open the door, unloosing the dank, musty smell of the house as though it were some half-inhabited cave. I turned on the light in the hall but there was no power. It was too late to buy candles. I carried my luggage into the hall. I stayed with friends that night and spent the days until Christmas paying bills and trying to convince the electricity people to put back on the power and the telephone people to re-connect me and the newspaper to pay me in advance. I did not know that you came to Ireland for Christmas, and that you were in Dublin for some of those days, and that you stayed with friends of mine, people I introduced you to. I got on with things.

You will remember the house, the night I told you about it: how I owned another place, a house I had left empty and there was a bed there, and a cooker and electricity. But no bathroom and an outside toilet. I had never slept there until we went there together. You preferred it to the flat I had in Harcourt Terrace, I think.

Now I was back in this house, and it was cold. I worked hard, wrote as much as I could, until I was offered another job in another newspaper, and dis-covered that I could get a new contract to work four weeks on and four weeks off, and that meant that I could spend one month out of every two in Barcelona.

I cannot remember when we met again that year, or how it happened although I have desperately tried to piece it together. I might have some of the sequence wrong.

I remember trying to re-write passages of my novel in a flat in Trafalgar near Plaça Catalunya, and the phone ringing from my newspaper to tell me that there was a general election in Ireland, and would I come back to write about it. I didn't want to go back, but in the next few hours I started to think about Charlie Haughey and his ruling Fianna Fáil party and I rang back and said that I wouldn't need to come home, I could write about it now, from Barcelona, and I could fax it in the morning.

I worked on the piece all evening and again in the morning and on Sunday they used it on the op-ed page of the paper. From Barcelona it was easy to see things clearly, or imagine you did: how Haughey had manipu-lated the abortion and the divorce referenda; how he had no clear views or policies on the North or the economy;

how everything was subsumed into winning elections, into short-term gain.

I went back home to cover the election. I thought maybe I should keep away from Haughey for a while, so I went around Ireland on a helicopter with Alan Dukes, the leader of Fine Gael, the main opposition party. Dukes had a funny smug arrogance; he exuded intellectual and moral superiority. If you aked him a question which included a statement ('You too, introduced health cuts while in government, didn't you?') he would immediately have to contradict you. He was slightly embarrassed by all the kissing of babies and posing for photographs. I remember vaguely disliking him and being half-sorry that I had attacked Haughey so vehemently. Now that I was back in Ireland things were not so simple.

I don't know how we got in touch that week, but on Friday when I had written my piece about Dukes I took the train to Galway and I met you there. Other friends came, the ones you had stayed with at Christmas. You and I slept in the same bed in a flat you had on the way to Salthill, although we did not talk about making commitments. I was so pleased to see you.

Sunday was a beautiful, clear, sunny day in the west of Ireland. We walked up by the river in Galway after brunch at the Quays and hired two rowing boats. There were maybe eight people altogether. And we rowed, shouting and laughing, towards the ruin of some castle. You were always at ease in big groups like that; you could keep control, know what to say. But when we arrived at the ruin the two of us moved away from the rest; we lay down on the grass together, close to each other, I rested my head against you and maybe we talked, or relaxed and said nothing, and maybe a wind blew across the water and a few people passed by and we could hear the others play-acting in the distance. But what I remember more than any of this are the words coming into my head 'This is the happiest I have been' and thinking the words were true.

We went back to Salthill and tried to get into the swimming pool but it was closed. I wanted to go for a swim in the sea. We hung around the waterfront at Salthill; there were fewer of us now, I think, but enough still to make a lot of noise. Someone started to sing Dusty Springfield, or Bette Midler, and all of you knew all the words. People looked at us as they passed. And then:

> *I want to be Bobby's girl*
> *I want to be Bobby's girl*
> *That's the most important thing for me.*

I wondered as I stood there, half-joining in, laughing at the fun of this, what would happen if the Fine Gael helicopter were suddenly to land, and all the journalists and politicians looked out.

> *And if I was Bobby's girl*
> *If I was Bobby's girl*
> *What a faithful, thankful girl I'd be!*

Where was my interest in health-spending as a percentage of GNP? My views on integrity in politics? The dead serious and moralistic tone? All gone now, put into storage.

Two of us went for a swim, myself and Gerry McNamara, in the tame Atlantic of Galway Bay. It was freezing. I remember how aware I was of getting older as I stripped down to my togs. I spoke to Gerry about it recently. He remembered the boat trip and the singing (Dionne Warwick and the Andrews Sisters), but he felt a sort of freedom and ease about going into the sea with everyone watching him and he thought that I did too.

I left Galway the next day, which was a Bank Holiday. I took the train for Dublin. You stayed behind. I was due in Limerick at eight o'clock on Tuesday morning to have breakfast with Des O'Malley, the leader of the Progressive Democrat Party. Once more, I was going to have to become serious-minded, locate the part of myself that I had kept in abeyance all weekend, that you knew nothing about. You had no interest in the minutiae of politics, or the strange systems of the Republic of Ireland, and because we never talked about it much, you had a right perhaps to feel that it was something I did for the money, or to distract myself from other, more important things.

It was a Bank Holiday but when I checked the train timetables I checked them for Sunday and thus I missed the train to Limerick. I realized as I stood in the station that I would miss Des O'Malley who had agreed that I could travel alone with him and his driver through his constituency all day Tuesday. The early-morning train would be too late.

It was still a beautiful warm evening. I walked home, wondering what I would do. I phoned a taxi who said it would cost a hundred and twenty pounds to go to Limerick. I had the money; I realized that I should go. I would earn it on the O'Malley piece anyway. I couldn't face a night on my own here, caught between the self of the weekend and the self of the election.

I brought the Sunday papers with me, the ones I had not had time to read, and I sat in the back of the cab as we moved slowly south and I read about the progress of the election. The taxi driver did not speak, and soon the light began to fade, gently, softly. I watched the calm, red sunset in the western sky. We passed through the empty streets of provincial towns. The journey would take two and a half, maybe three, hours. Mount-mellick, Portlaoise, Thurles. The pubs were open and a few corner shops. The towns seemed oddly harmless places, like wisps of smoke, hardly there at all.

And after a while on that journey I began to feel an intense effortless happiness. It was different from the previous day with you in Galway where the phrase came into my head 'This is the happiest I have been' and I felt the power of the phrase. This was a sustained feeling: ease, well-being, happiness. Maybe driving across Ireland on a summer's night induces happiness. There was still light in the sky. I had all the comfort and afterglow of the days with you, and I knew somewhere – maybe not that night, maybe it was afterwards I realized it – that I was happier in the afterglow than I was at the time.

Des O'Malley in the morning was solemn and stiff. Taking me with him in the car was part of the terrible purgatory of elections. He didn't smile. His wife smiled. I had met both of them before, Pat his wife was easier to get on with. He spoke with a determined, unrhetorical edge to his tone, a politician who had missed out on the glorious high-spending days of the sixties, and had become a connoisseur of retrenchment. I wondered what we were going to talk about in the car. I didn't know much about retrenchment.

As far as I remember we did not talk at all. We stopped regularly so he could meet his constituents, and then got into the car and drove to the next village. I asked him if he played golf, and he said he did. But since I knew nothing about golf, then I couldn't think what to ask him next. I said nothing and he seemed content enough – while remaining tense – as we drove around the constituency.

Later, we went back to his house. His wife was there again and a friend of the O'Malleys whom I also knew well. Des O'Malley changed completely once he went into his own house. He laughed a lot and made jokes with his children. He suggested to his son that he go and do some study, and for one moment he sounded like his old self until I realized he was mocking himself and his son was laughing at him. I was pleased as I sat there watching him that he had two selves as well. Maybe everyone does, I thought. Or maybe only politicians and me.

We drove to Dublin and as we passed the prison in Portlaoise where the IRA are held I said to him: 'You started that prison, didn't you?' (He was Minister for Justice in the early seventies.) 'I did,' he said in a voice half-weary, half-melancholy. I did not know what to make of him.

I went back to Barcelona and you arrived in the city soon afterwards. I remember you telephoning from the airport on a Sunday morning; we met in the Café de la Ópera. You went to Sitges, lay on the beach and enjoyed the swimming and I went to Menorca and I still cannot remember why. I flew there in the early morning and I was shocked at the bare, windswept landscape and the dry stone walls. I had always wanted to take the boat back from Mahon to Barcelona, the boat that leaves in the morning and spends all day sailing across the Mediterranean, maybe that is why I went. I dreamed of lying on deck beside the swimming pool under the pure luxury of the blue sky.

But it wasn't like that. It was one of those strange choppy days, the sky all grey. There was no question of lying on deck as the boat began to rock against the waves. We arrived two hours late in the port of Barcelona. You were waiting, and sometimes you could be wonderful when we met like that from planes or trains, you were so warm, in such good humour, and you had psyched yourself up to have a big fancy meal and drinks, just the two of us, and I was so down, my stomach sick, all I wanted to do was go to bed.

Weather. Mostly, the days were scorching. I loved being indoors on August days in Barcelona, with a small stream of air floating through the house, reading or writing or doing nothing. I loved the humid air, and the half-deserted city, just as you loved the beach and the sea. I loved the city bars at night; how people had to walk slowly in the hot city; how people never got enough sleep in this heat, and had to do everything carefully, slowly.

One night it began to rain in Sitges, a sudden, fierce downpour. We were in a bar and we walked back in the rain towards the apartment you had rented until we were soaked. It was late and there was no one around. We were walking by the sea and it was easy then to slip off our clothes and jump into the half-warm water, leaving our clothes on the sand to soak even more. And when we got out of the sea the thunder and lightning started, lightning like you see in the movies, and we stood there loving it all, and that was happiness too, especially since we knew that home was nearby, and there we could dry ourselves and fall asleep together.

You left Barcelona at the end of another summer, and once more I stayed on. I started another novel. A new government was formed in Ireland; Haughey was Taoiseach and Des O'Malley was Minister for Industry and Commerce. But industry and commerce had come to a standstill in Ireland. I stayed with you in London that autumn and we happened one Saturday evening to be driving with your brother through Kilburn and I said I'd love to go to an Irish pub. You were both a bit puzzled, but you agreed and we stopped and had something to eat and then went into a pub. We had a drink in the lounge first at the table beside a father and his son. The father had an Irish accent, the son an English accent. There was a softness about both of them in the way they made space for us. But they didn't speak much to us or to each other: the emigrant and his son trying to have a drink together on a Saturday night.

The bar was wild with the new Irish emigrants. There was an Irish band, and the music was much too loud. I had not been in Ireland for some time, and I was suddenly moved by all these Irish faces, and the way people spoke to each other, attentive and warm. Suddenly, I wanted to go home. I went to get a drink and when I came back I noticed how frantic the music was, how frantic the drinking, and the sense of desperation mixed in with all this energy and innocence. And when I turned to speak to you I noticed tears in your eyes. You had been watching the scene too: people far from home on a Saturday night, who would soon be turned out of this cocoon into Kilburn, people whom Ireland had no jobs for, no place for. Our compatriots. But maybe they were all fine, having a good time, maybe we saw something of ourselves in those faces.

When the winter came I went back to Dublin. The house was done up now, walls knocked down, gas central heating installed, floors sanded and varnished, walls painted white, bookshelves, paintings. A bathroom even. Sometimes we talked late at night on the phone. We were both seeing other people, and that seemed reasonable, and we were even able to discuss it on the line between Dublin and London.

But you came to Dublin again at Christmas and I remember meeting on a freezing cold evening in a pub in Parkgate Street, and us going back to my house and lighting a fire. Something had happened. When we went to bed together there was no desire, just warmth and closeness. And we spent hours like that. And there were parties and gatherings. One evening we were having dinner before we went out, there was good food and wine and we were both well scrubbed and dressed. When the phone rang it was a voice I did not recognize asking for you. I did not mean to stay and listen, but by the time I realized it was your new lover it was too late, and I did not enjoy listening to the way you spoke to him. And a few minutes after you put down the phone it rang again, and this time it was for me. We finished the wine and telephoned a taxi to take us to the party. We laughed about the phone calls. We knew that we had blown it.

CHRISTOPHER HOPE

1988

The Year I Went Home

A painting bought by Christopher Hope in Moscow in 1988.
The message reads:
'Comrade! What are you doing for perestroika?'

I WENT TO MOSCOW in 1988 and things were never the same again. For the first time, since leaving Africa for Europe, I found myself in a European capital where the ruling caste was unabashedly corrupt, enthusiastically hypocritical, privileged people with their own shops, hospitals, schools and ghettos. While pretending to be the finest place on earth, this utopia subjected its citizens to many doleful humiliations. It imprisoned, exiled and destroyed many who disagreed with it, and bored the rest to distracted fury.

The rulers in Moscow called themselves communists. But I knew them for who they were. My brothers, sisters, cousins from South Africa, better adapted to the cold northern winters, perhaps, and with a fondness for fine fur hats and vodka, but my family none the less. How strangely familiar to a South African. In short, in 1988, I set off for a foreign capital, and found I had come home.

There was one important difference. Everyone was beastly about the South African ruling caste. Fewer dared to be beastly about Russian rulers, lest they rise up and smite the mockers with their intercontinental ballistic weapons. And the Russians had a few other things in their favour in 1988. They had Mikhail Gorbachev. They had something called Perestroika. And they had Glasnost. Elements of the Russian trinity which were spoken of very highly within the Western press.

So I travelled full of expectation. I arrived at the Ukraina Hotel in Moscow, a huge pile built in a style described as Stalin rococo, or Soviet Gothic. A towering and gloomy edifice with spires and turrets, ornamented with hammers and sickles. Where nothing and no one worked. Where the staff repeated, at regular intervals, the mantra of those supplying service in such Soviet detention centres for tourists – a single sombre response to all requests and enquiries: 'Go to your room and wait.'

I went looking for something called 'Perestroika', the much-advertised Russian programme of reform. I talked to members of the ruling party in their schools, special shops and select apartment blocks. They could not help me. I asked people I met in the hospitals. I spoke to hookers and black-market currency dealers. They shrugged their shoulders. I asked Alya, a hooker, a girl built like a blonde, plump and sticky spider in white boots who plied for trade near the Ukraina Hotel. Alya laughed. I spoke to Russians late at night in the privacy of their small kitchens where, I soon learnt, they were most likely to let their hair down and talk freely. They responded with looks of pain, they became embarrassed, or bored.

After a few weeks of fruitless enquiry I travelled back to the West. In London I found everyone knew about Perestroika. The newspapers were full of it. The

Americans approved of it. And they approved of Mikhail Gorbachev. He was a regular guy. A decent sort. The Russians were lucky to have him. His wife used a credit card on foreign shopping trips. They would vote for him, if only they had the chance. If he ran for President, he could win.

So I went back to Moscow for another spell, and tried again. If this thing called Perestroika existed, then changes were happening somewhere. And if I applied myself conscientiously, then these changes would disclose themselves. Because many experts in the West had assured the world that Perestroika did indeed exist. That it was good and strong and powerful. If the Russians did not see it, then perhaps they did not deserve to have this thing called Perestroika. Surely they did not deserve to have Mikhail Gorbachev. Perhaps they were stuck in the past and simply did not realize that these were modern times? This was 1988, after all. And there were huge changes taking place in the USSR. Life was very much better. It said so, in our newspapers.

It was all very curious. We knew the Russians were all-powerful in the matter of missiles. But I sat in my hotel bedroom and wondered about the electric plugs. If you sent a man around the moon and you could destroy half the planet at the touch of a button, why could you not get your plugs to work? Or make enough soap to go round? Above all, why did the place seem so clearly to be on its last legs? Why was the CIA spending billions spying on the USSR? Why did they not send an agent to the Ukraina Hotel for a week? Why did they not ask one of their people to walk the streets, and stand in the vodka queues?

It was all very puzzling. My Russian friends enjoyed my bewilderment, in that icy and perverse Russian spirit of coldly relishing what damaged them. The spirit often revealed itself as a strange hauteur – a scornful indifference marked by a dismissive shrug. But the indifference, I learnt, was deceptive. Russians cared – they cared so much that only glacial contempt made things bearable. A form of anaesthetic. They had spent so long being lied to by powerful idiots that they had developed a kind of frozen numbness. A talent for appearing not to notice. 'If you think this is bad,' they said with pride as they led me through the circles of Moscow life, 'then come with us.'

I learnt the principle by which to proceed. The usual Russian maxim was 'Anything not permitted is forbidden.' Everything beyond the narrow confines of the official tour, policed by Intourist girls and their red hankies with their irritable lassoing of footloose foreigners, to the obedient businessmen in search of Soviet profits (surely a contradiction if ever there was one) – all this was out of bounds. So if you proceeded on the reverse principle that 'everything not expressly forbidden is permitted', then no one thought to question your right to be present at secret meetings of evangelical Christians. Or visiting a monastery which had once housed orphans of the politically condemned, whose early-morning prayer was to thank the State and Stalin for the very air they breathed. Or at a party of Hell's Angels. Or at a meeting in a café with no name, where there gathered the only three punks in Moscow.

Everything was forbidden, but all seemed possible. It was the Russian paradox. You conceded to those who ran the country that they had the power to tell you what to do. After that it was up to you to do as you liked.

In each of the seasons I returned to Moscow. In the spring of 1988 I witnessed Russians labouring in maternity wards to bring new Muscovites into the world. I followed the children to school. I visited the Palace of Weddings and watched the instructional video preparing young couples for the brief civil marriage ceremony to come. And I waved when the rusty nuptial Zil limousine drew up at the front door of the Palace of Weddings and carried off another bridal pair to the small apartment they would share with their parents-in-law.

I learnt the importance of always carrying an empty bag and buying anything on offer. From shoes to oranges. Who knew when the windfall would come again? While Western spectators in liberal societies watched television pictures of Mikhail Gorbachev being cheered to the echo in capital cities, I watched a South American soap opera, a lurid tale Russians doted on. Steamy love among slaves and plantation owners brought much of Moscow to a stop several mornings a week. I learnt never to mention the word Perestroika in polite company. I visited one of the few homes for the elderly, where Russians without families waited for death. And I called at the Moscow morgue and understood what my friends meant when they told me that if there was one thing worse than living in the Soviet Union, it was dying there. For dying created bureaucratic problems of transport and interment even more difficult to solve than the daily struggle for bread and shelter.

Above all, I was happy. My Russian friends gave me a country to put in place of the country I felt I had lost. 'Why do we live like this?' went the grimly gentle enquiry. 'As a warning to others not to follow our example.'

But they did better than this. Despite a government which had treated its citizens as not very bright ten-year-olds, my friends had somehow resisted the pressure to conform to governmental definition. Their spirit of resistance was not one that ruled out being crushed by the system. But it gave bleak warning that there was no limit to the number of times it could be crushed, and still survive. No one expected things to alter radically. That was seen as a fond, Western illusion, adhered to by politicians and intellectuals in the liberal democracies, places as distant to most Russians as the distant galaxies.

When I returned to the West, from time to time, and drew pictures of my visits to Moscow I encountered bafflement and dismay. I remember the editor of an American journal asking if he could publish some of my sketches. So I sent him glimpses of the bitter gaiety to be found in the vodka queues and the Palace of Weddings and the cemeteries of Moscow. He returned them with an offended note explaining that they were 'far too negative for the times'. I talked to German academics and was roundly censured by a Professor of Russian Studies for my scant solidarity with well-meaning reformers of the left.

It might have been enough to make me weep. Except for the fact that in 1988 I went to Moscow. And I learnt there that some things were enough to make you laugh.

ROBERT McLIAM WILSON

1989

Incendiary Belfast rearranged by Maguire and Paterson

THERE'S A PICTURE of me then, standing still in some small Oxford breeze, looking pretty English. I was twenty-five, which was fine. I wore someone else's jacket and found a fit. Early that spring, the sun shone impossible and I knew it would be that kind of year.

I stood on Charing Cross Road, as bright drizzle sputtered itself out. A roofless youth offered me a blowjob for a packet of cigarettes. Cambridge Circus and all its little joys. I looked at my feet as I declined. It seemed to me that London had gone all wrong.

There was a government that seemed to be selling the country off. They didn't seem to like us much. We continued to elect them as they continued to throw it all away. It's bad enough to shit in your hat but why then proceed to put it on your head.

And that's when it all started going wrong. All the people who'd made the money lost the money. The poor people hadn't made any money but even they managed to lose some too. That had been called trickledown economics. But all those kinds of dreams ended and people woke up to a very pale decade-end.

I didn't like to say that I'd told you so.

There was a lot of trickledown happening in Eastern Europe. The masses revolted. A bit. It all worked out.

The gun stuff didn't seem to happen as much as it might have and that was good, if surprising. I'd lived in Belfast and I knew about that gun stuff.

This made some people excessively optimistic about the new private heart of people. It looked like there'd been a change in us, a way might be found to liberate us bloodlessly from all our thralls. Seemed unlikely to me. I knew how much we all really liked the right to fight and kill. I started a countdown to the next big war.

None the less, life was most undystopian. To walk a street in 1989 was to walk a street in my personal year twenty-five. There is an idea that youth is wasted on the young. Not on me it's not. I know it's good stuff, this youth.

When I walk (soft light, mist and mountain), the street seems springy and youthful. The tarmac is blue in the light and the very road is transfigured. Boy, it feels good to walk. I really appreciate youth, that juicy stuff. When I breathe with particular ease, cross a road in trim bounds or walk an easy roadmile, I revel in it. I realize I'm enjoying something temporary and I make the most of it. I take tape recordings of my youth, testimony from expert witnesses. I love the way things look, sound, weigh and feel to me. I'm a connoisseur of youth.

Best of all though is the secret conviction youth gives you. I couldn't take too much too seriously because, good or bad, I always knew in both my hearts that something good was going to happen.

It was all just England, neutral, comforting, heart-stoppingly, spine-chillingly moderate.

I stood in the lamplit street while neon blared. I watched the girls walk in their high heels, looking good enough to eat – meals on heels. I watched the men walk, the seeking bachelors and the married rogues, high in sensible arts. Everybody seemed to know where they were going. That impressed me.

And then there was the Swimming Girl. I loved her. She could talk underwater. She had a dress with buttons down the back (interesting how men always remember women's garments by their means of access). Twenty-five was just one year too late to ignore the compulsions of tenderness, compassion and benevolence. I tried all that for size.

Got myself published. A good friend gave me the recipe for staying ahead of the competition:

'It's not, Fuck now – work later,' he said. 'Nor is it, Work now – fuck later. No, it is in fact, Work now – work later.'

I had lived in England for six years. I liked the English. I was the Catholic Irishman who thought the English were all right. It was the way they had housed, fed, clothed and educated me all those years. Thanks folks, I was pretty expensive.

Attracted by the idea of an Irishman who didn't like

the Irish, the BBC asked me to make a film about Belfast, my home town. Sharpened some knives and packed my bags.

I got on a plane flown by an American pilot who didn't know the way (I swear). So for once we flew over the city itself. It looked small and flat there by the sea and so delicate and so lovely. The sky was like litmus paper, strips of indigo, violet and turquoise.

And I went back to Belfast. Sometimes, Belfast can look like the past, remote or recent (the confident Protestant past). Burgher Belfast and all its little histories. I had some histories of my own there.

And well, northern winter mornings are just so exciting. You look out of a window stained with condensation, your fingers already losing the stored heat of sleep. The sky is pale white, wet and cold. People on the streets already rush and hurry as though something momentous is happening (they are just moving to keep warm). They are wrapped and marvellous. The trees are leafless and intricate as webs. The air is as sharp and fresh as cold beer.

And the half-arsed, half-dressed kids you see in the movies all do strut that stuff of theirs here. Short back and sides, knees and elbows, sticks and stones (which do, as a matter of fact, break their bones).

That's why the Irish justify cliché as their art form. It's all they've got. In Belfast, cliché isn't cliché – it's the cutting edge.

I looked up some old friends. Difficult since so few

had stayed in the city that had grown them. There had been a few deaths too. I'd been away such a short time and look at what had happened. Two suicides, a car crash (with new wife and baby), a heart condition and a solitary episode of ordinance.

Marty had been the existentialist at my school. Middle-class but scruffy, Marty hadn't liked football or fighting. That made Marty existentialist. Can't think of a better reason for such a reputation.

Marty had stopped existing two years earlier. He was passing an Army checkpoint which was attacked with crudely made mortar bombs. Four of the six bombs failed to explode but one of the bombs exploded on Marty's windscreen and Marty had stopped existing. Two of the soldiers had stopped existing too. They had been standing four feet apart. The last bomb landed between and did bad stuff to them. Somebody else lost a leg or two but continued existing.

I brushed up my schedule. Worked out that I could make that film and be outa there in six weeks.

Six weeks later, I walked the coast of Belfast, concrete and crane, the docks thick with the quality of the sea. Something happened to me which I still can't understand. Ten years and thousands of pounds' worth of charitable education had helped me surrender my birthright (feeling it the elegant thing to do under the circumstances). Here I was coming over all Mick. It was Arran jumpers and shillelaghs next.

As always, there was music in my head. I had made

my film in Belfast. I had hoped to prove what a fucking shithole it was. After six weeks there, I was moving in and getting myself all married.

And they shot a man in Derriaghy. Twice in the head when he answered his front door. I watched TV as his wife cried at the funeral. Hers was a strange noise, not human – surrendering to the impossible horror of what had happened, suitable, I thought. The only just and measured response to prevailing circumstances.

And they apologized. They had killed the wrong man and they apologized. I had forgotten that they did that.

I had also forgotten that in Belfast, people place bunches of flowers on the spots where people are murdered. The city is often dotted with these false little gardens. The flowers bright and new in their wrapping paper, or faded and dog-eared with age. Any long walk through the city takes you past one or more of these spots. If the flowers are old, you pass and wonder who died there. You *always* fail to remember.

But then it seemed that a mood settled over the city like some faint drizzle of compromise – a hint that the dealings we dealt could involve some idea of otherness not necessarily to be shot at or exploded.

An idea was born and dead that day – the intelligent poet, the moderate Irishman, the honest politician – it lasted the hours between ten-thirty in the morning and the local news bulletins at one o'clock but that was an augustan period in itself.

I'd seen the shape of political optimism in Northern Ireland. There was a future there.

On the eve of Christmas Eve that year, I was married in Belfast City Hall. We were both dressed in black and the men on the door directed us to the funerals department. We had two witnesses. They gave us an alibi. One wedding photograph. We stand in our sable under a poster which read: 'Belfast still says no' – some bits just write themselves.

Near four years later and I'm still here.

You see, Belfast can make its citizens feel like big people, epic and tremendous. The city has a remnant of grandeur that no poverty or violence can finally dent. There are times when the city adopts postures which no one who does not live here can see or understand. Postures which do not involve ordinance or ballistics or brutality. At eight in the morning in May, the sky goes as blue as it ever will and you have to close your eyes at the brightness. At night, when it rains straight, Belfast can feel diluvian, apocalyptic.

Sometimes when the day is late and the sun is low and orange with age, the city looks so light that you could blow it away. The multiple windows of Belfast's dwarf skyscrapers turn red in pairs like there's a fire inside. Between the trees dogs redden in the sudden blush of sun.

And when summer comes, Belfast is the possible itself. The city fills with pale people turning uncertainly brown and the jumbled noise of holiday radio songs. It moves me to drive home late on a Saturday night when the girls are out barelegged in short skirts and the boys are wearing linen trousers stained by their beer, and innocent Belfast lies bemused and strewn with their drunken litter and everyone labours under the misconception that I drive a taxi.

I'm still here. And in the broad night the sirens whoop and chatter like metallic married couples. We're talking about spilt beer, we're talking about the end of the world. It's not yet ideal, old Belfast. We're still shouting and bombing and whining and dying. But it's all right, don't worry – because I know.

I *still* know that something good is going to happen.

NORMAN LEWIS

1990

*Namek
and the
Smoked Ancestor*

Norman Lewis in Irianjaya

T HE ONE THING that impressed me about the airport building at Wamena was an enormous artificial flower placed in the path of arriving passengers. This, a four-foot-across polystyrene Rafflesia, had been so painstakingly created that for a moment I thought I detected a sickly floral fragrance in its vicinity, whereas the fact was that the airport as a whole smelt of nothing but a powerful anti-mosquito spray in use. After the flower came the information desk where I enquired for a taxi driver, who according to a Jayapura agent could usually be found at the airport, who was the only Dani in Wamena who spoke English reasonably well. I was taken to the back of the building, where he was pointed out to me, occupied with some tourists who were photographing him in national garb. He was short for a Dani, with glittering eyes and a black beard, and as he hurried forward at the end of the session to introduce himself his limp translated itself into a skip. His flat, fur hat, of the kind once worn by Henry Tudor, enhanced a dignity by no means impaired by his nakedness. Apart from this head-covering he wore nothing but a two-foot yellow penis gourd, referred to in Wamena as a *koteka*, held in the upright position by a string round the waist. The scrotum had been tucked away at the base of this, exposing the testicles in a neat, blueish sac. This did not surprise me, for as the plane

taxied in I had noticed a half-dozen naked men unload-
ing a cargo plane.

We shook hands. Namek repeated the greeting '*weh,
weh*' (welcome) a number of times, excused himself and
came back wearing ill-fitting ex-army jungle fatigues. It
now turned out that the taxi, in which he had a quarter
share, was the magnificent ruin of an ancient Panhard-
Levasseur, formerly owned by a Javanese rajah, which
now awaited us, refulgent with polished brass, at the
airport gate. In this we travelled in some state to a
losmen he recommended where I took the austere room
offered for one night, then after a quick tidy-up joined
him in a species of porch, opening on to the street,
where we discussed the possibilities of an investigatory
trip into the interior.

By chance we had arrived in the midst of a minor
crisis. The town had been showered overnight by large
flying insects which, although harmless, were of men-
acing appearance. Many of them had found their way
into the *losmen*, where they hurtled noisily across rooms
and down passages, colliding with staff and guests, and
then, their energy exhausted, were added to the piles
into which they had been swept, until time could be
found to clear them away. Namek took a gloomy view
of this phenomenon, promising, he assured me, a
change in the weather, which was likely to be for the
worse.

'How do you come to speak English so well?' I
asked him.

'My mother was killed in an accident and a Catholic father adopted me,' he said. 'From him I am learning English and Dutch.' He spoke in a soft sing-song, eyes lowered, as if soothing a child, then looking up suddenly at the end of each sentence for assent.

'Now I am a registered guide,' he said. 'No other taxi has assurance. Also I work in my garden. Tomorrow I will bring you sweet potatoes.'

'Are you married?'

'I have two wives,' he said. 'My father had two handfuls. That is the way we say for ten. We are always counting on fingers.' He raised his eyes to mine with a quick, furtive smile. 'You see we are going downhill.'

'Catholic, are you?'

'In Wamena all Catholics.'

'Doesn't your priest object to the wives?'

'For Danis they are making special rules. It's OK for them to have many wives. I cannot catch up with my father. Times now changed. Maybe one day I will have one wife more. That is enough.'

There was a moment of distraction while the *losmen*'s cat raced through over the furniture in chase of the last of the fearsome insects. Namek showed me the agent's letter to him. 'My friend says you are wanting to see of our country. May I know of your plans?'

'I haven't any,' I said. 'This is just a quick trip to get the feeling of the place. What ought I to see? Merauke – Sorong? The Asmat, would you say?'

'You may show me your *surat jalan*. Did you put down these places?'

'I only put down the Baliem. Can the others be added here?'

'No. For that you must go back to Jayapura for permission to go to these places.'

'In Jakarta they said it could be done here.'

'They are wrong. Go to the police office and they will tell you.'

'It seems a waste of time. Let us suppose I go back – am I sure of getting the permissions?'

'Here nothing is sure. One day they are telling you yes, the next day they say no. They will not agree to tell you on telephone. Now also the telephone is not working.'

'So what do you suggest?'

He was reading the *surat jalan*, going over the words, letter by letter, with the tip of his forefinger, each word spoken softly, identified, and its meaning confirmed.

'With this *surat jalan* you may go to Karubaga,' he said.

'And what has Karubaga to offer?'

'Scenery very good. Also you are seeing different things. There are women in Karubaga turning themselves into bats.'

'That's promising,' I said. 'How do we get there?'

'By Mérpati plane,' he said. 'To come back we are walking five days. In Karubaga you may find one porter. Maybe two. Also one bodyguard.'

'Why the bodyguard? Cannibals?'

The thick beard drew away from his lips as he humoured me with a smile. 'No cannibals. Sometimes unfriendly people.'

The many frustrations of travel on impulse had left their brand-mark of caution on me. 'What are the snags?' I asked. 'Tell me the worst.'

'Very much climbing,' he said. 'Heart must be strong. *Surat* to be stamped by police in five villages. At Bakondini no river-bridge. Porters may bring you on their backs across, or rattan bridge to be built one day, two days – no more. Every day now it is raining a little.' As he spoke a shadow fell across us. Part of the porch was of glass, and through it I saw that where a patch of blue sky had shown only a few minutes before, black, muscled cloud masses had formed and were writhing and twisting like trapped animals. A single clap of thunder set off a cannonade of reverberations through the echoing clap-board of the town, morning became twilight, and then we heard the rain clattering towards us over the thousand tin roofs of Wamena. Pigs and dogs were sprinting down the street, chased by a frothing current, then disappearing behind a fence of water.

The rain stopped, the sun broke through, and the steam rose in ghostly, tattered shapes from all the walls and pavements of the town. Mountain outlines, sharp-edged and glittering, surfaced in the clear sky above the fog. 'In one hour all dry again,' Namek said. We came back to the question of travel. 'I'll think about Karu-baga,' I said. 'Any suggestions about using up the afternoon?'

'We may go to Dalima to visit my smoked ancestor,' Namek said. 'For this we may bring with us American cigarettes.'

In Wamena they smoked clove cigarettes, and there was a long search in the market for the prized American kind that were rarely offered for sale. By the time we found a few packets, the shallow floods had already dried away, and we set off. We chugged away on three cylinders into the mountains to the north, left the car sizzling and blowing steam at Uwosilimo, and trudged five miles up a path to Dalima. In these off-the-beaten-track places the Dani had held on to their customs until the last moment, cropping ears and amputating fingers years after such exaggerated expressions of bereavement following the deaths of close relatives had been stamped out elsewhere. Persons of great power and influence, known as *kain koks*, were not cremated in the usual way but smoked over a slow fire for several months and thereafter hung from the eaves of their houses, where they continued to keep a benevolent eye on the community for decades, even centuries, until the newly arrived Indonesians launched their drive against 'barbarous practices', took down the offending cadavers and burned them or threw them into the river.

Namek's ancestor had been one of the few success-fully hidden away, and now, in a slightly relaxed atmosphere, he could be discreetly produced for the admiration of visitors with access to cigarettes from the USA, which he let it be known through a shaman was the offering he most appreciated.

The whole village turned out for us in holiday mood, the women topless and in their best grass skirts, and the men in the local style of penis gourds, with feathers dangling from their tips. We distributed cigarettes and the current *kain kok* tottered into view, overwhelmingly impressive with the boar's tusks curving from the hole in his septum, his bird-of-paradise plumes, and his valuable old shells. Beaming seraphically he punched a small hole in the middle of a cigarette and began to smoke it at both ends. He was the possessor of four handfuls of wives, and of this Namek said in a sibilant aside, 'Now he is old, and his women play their games while they are working in the fields.'

With this the smoked ancestor was carried out, having been crammed for this public appearance into a Victorian armchair. One arm was flung high into the air, a malacca cane grasped in the hand, while the other hand, reaching surreptitiously down behind his back, held the polished skull of a bird. The Tudor-style hat affected by all the clan's leading males was tilted jauntily over an eye socket, and the ancestor's skin was quite black and frayed and split like the leather of an ancient sofa. His jaws had been wrenched wide apart by the fumigant, and now the old *kain kok* lit a Chesterfield, puffed on it, and wedged it between the two molar teeth that remained. Behind him descendants of lesser importance awaited their turn to make similar offerings to the ancestor.

The scene was in part grotesque but abounding in good cheer. The women rushed at us giggling and happy to show off their mutilated hands, and the men seemed proud of the tatters of skin which were all that remained of their ears. The village was a handsome one, scrupulously clean and well kept, and I was fascinated to see that the villagers had uprooted trees in the jungle and replanted them in such a way that they drooped trusses of fragrant yellow blossoms over the thatches of their houses. These attracted butterflies of sombre magnificence, which fed on the nectar until they became intoxicated and then toppled about the place like planes out of control, and were chased ineffectively both by the children and the village dog. In such Dani communities it is more or less share and share alike, and it seemed that in the allocation every child over the age of seven had been given a half-cigarette. These they were puffing at vigorously, and the village was full of the sound of their jubilation.

KATHY LETTE

1991

Dear Picador,

Many happy returns . . . oops. Maybe *not*. Let's start again. Happy birthday! I'm sorry I can't make a birthday contribution. Oh, once I could have. Once I could have written a pun-in-cheek, tongue-in-chic little piece that went straight for the jocular vein . . . But not now. Not since 1991. Since 1991 I haven't been able to use a word with more than two syllables in it. Well, I did once. The word was tranquillizer.

Once I could have written about any one of my regular, run-of-the-mill exploits: the most suitable sun-block to wear whilst bungy-jumping, nude, at Beachy Head; what to do when you find yourself inhaling the halitosis of a tiger shark you've swum too close to in the Caribbean; the best technique for the dislodgement of your gold necklace from the fly of a world famous guitarist . . . but not since 1991. Since 1991 the highlight of my day has been getting the lint out of the drier. Now you're lucky if you can get a complete sentence out of . . . And even then there is no guarantee that the sentence straight come out will. And even if it does, I'm more than likely to repeat everything twice repeat everything twice.

It could be sleep deprivation. It's a form of torture in some countries. There is a reason for this. It works. Right now I'd confess to anything . . . apart from the fact that there's nothing to confess to – except making space helmets out of old loo rolls and regularly rescuing the goldfish from the food disposal unit.

See Mother. See Mother run. See Mother save the little bitty goldfish. Bad insinkerator.

You see, 1991 was my first year of motherhood.

See Mother. See Mother cry. See Mother opening Valium bottle. See Mother swallowing all the pretty pink pills.

The trouble with motherhood is that you get the baby, but no Owner's Manual.

While the rest of the world was preoccupied with the Mother of all Battles, I was obsessed with the battle of all mothers. Oh, how I empathized with those soldiers in the Gulf. The intense boredom . . . punctuated with moments of acute fear. The *bottle*-fatigue. But let me move from the General (Stormin' Norman in this case) to the particular . . .

The shell-shock began with the birth itself. Put it this way, lying there with my legs in stirrups, a gloom of doctors wielding scalpels around my groin, adoption started to look like a very civilized alternative. It's Stone Age what you go through. It's prehistoric. How can this happen to women at the tail-end of the twentieth century? . . . To women who have portable phones and personal computers and sign up for lectures on 'Sexual Harassment in the Work Place'?

All those wasted hours attending No-Drugs-And-Squat-Earth-Mother classes . . . People had given me not the facts but the *fiction* of life. I now think of natural childbirth the way I think of natural appendectomy. I mean, would you go to the dentist's and say, 'I've got to have my tooth out. Let's do it *naturally*?' If, like me, you need a Mogodon to go to the dental surgery, *just for fluoride*, then forget the bean-bags, the breathing, the Le Boyeur. Just opt for the Full-Epidural-Wake-Me-When-It's-Over-And-The-Hairdresser's-Here approach.

The only natural thing about my childbirth was that I didn't have time to shave my legs first.

But this whole, hideous sexist joke does have a punchline – the little bundle of edible, tightly swaddled loveliness the midwife places in your arms at the end of it all. As the Allies went to war, January 1991 found me high on a heady cocktail of endorphins. From the Metropolitan Police wheel-clamping squad to Saddam Hussein, I wanted to mother them all.

Along with an entire menagerie of stuffed vermin in frilly frocks and striped pyjamas, a well-wisher gave me one of those *Mother and Baby's First Year* books. Flicking through the pristine calendar pages, I thrilled to the prospect of being the Perfect Mother with the Perfect Off-spring. I pictured myself running huge corporations by day and doing creative things with play-dough by night. I would bake wholemeal loaves and purée tofu and never miss a 6 a.m. rowing practice . . .

As I now flick back through this tome, I see that my first diary entry was a vow never to become one of those harried, hair-netted types who yelled and slapped and emotionally blackmailed . . .

Reading on, I find that by February, I'm yelling, smacking and emotionally blackmailing – mainly the tall, haggard streak of misery with bags under his eyes big enough to take on a world cruise, whom I vaguely recognize as the man I married. As Desert Storm raged in the background, I mentally added my husband to the casuality list.

By March I'm completely brain-dead. This could have something to do with the fact that I'm a twenty-four-hour catering service. Meals on Heels.

April and May go by in a blur of body fluids. Haven't encountered so much vomit since I was trapped in a tube carriage with a scrum of victorious Arsenal supporters.

July is ringed in red. Not because of the impending collapse of Communism in Russia. This was a landmark month because at twenty-eight weeks Baby should be sleeping through the night . . . Of course, this will only happen if you are a Celebrity Author of a 'Good Parenting Guide'. You know, the sort who promote politically correct nursery rhymes – 'Vertically Challenged Bo Peep' and 'Experientially Enhanced Mother Hubbard' . . .

As I continued to yo-yo in and out of bed night after night, summoned by the bonsai insomniac in the nursery next door – I became an expert on pre-dawn television. And there they were, the same Celebrity

Parents, gushing like the Kuwaiti oil-fields about early signs of genius in their off-spring. July's diary entry dwindled into a vow never to become one of those mothers who boasts, 'Ooh, he's advanced.'

By August, Baby first crawls . . . up the stairs with the babysitter in his mouth. Feral behaviour is not supposed to start until at least two. 'Ooh,' spouse and I enthuse to each other, 'he's advanced.'

Late August pre-dawn TV brings news that Mother Russia has Post-Glasnost-Depression and looks set to commit infanticide.

By September, Baby takes his first steps – on to the third-floor window ledge. Red Adair's antics pale in comparison.

By October, I'm broke. The tooth fairy, I'll have you know, takes bank cards by now. For months the only thing I've written are cheques. It strikes me that there could be a vague connection between the prolificacy of Jane Austen, George Eliot, Virginia Woolf, the Brontës, Edith Sitwell, Dorothy Parker, Lillian Hellman, Simone de Beauvoir, and Co., and their lack of progeny . . . But am too tired to analyse this thought any further. I seem to keep falling asleep at inconvenient moments. Believe me, babies are a 100 per cent effective means of contraception. I'm also demented. One day I placed all the lethal household substances within reach and my toddler under the sink.

By November, I'm remembering how I pitied my childless girlfriends. I imagine them, poor creatures, as they laze on the decks of friends' yachts, anaesthetizing their sadness with Don Perignon and pâté. The deprived fools. Never to know the joys of projectile mucus. Never to be beaten to Mayfair in Monopoly. Never to know that poo can be a decorative option. November's entry concludes with a vow not to have another child, never, ever, ever . . .

By December I'm worrying about the Oedipal complex . . . Maybe I should have two . . . And what if they fight? Perhaps then three. And then, of course, a fourth to avoid the third-child-syndrome . . . But last children are spoilt rotten, which means having a fifth, sixth, seventh, eighth . . .

On New Year's Eve, 1991, while the New World Order celebrated peace on earth (for 'peace' read a pause for Saddam Hussein to breed more nuclear reactors) my spouse and I made paper Stealth bombers and Tornados out of the remaining pages of my *Mother and Baby's First Year* album and toasted our survival with a cup of tea. It was then he asked me how I'd like my eggs. I told him 'fertilized'.

See Father. See Father run! See Father run out of the house screaming.

My vow of no more babies turned out to be as fraudulent as the war-free promise of the New World Order. Here I am in 1993, forty weeks pregnant. Ridiculous cravings have set in . . . such as for a cease-fire in Yugoslavia. So now you know why I can't contribute a birthday piece. *Pre*-natal depression has me

in its grips. The first case known to medical science . . .
Talk about getting in before the rush.

My only advice to other mums-to-be is firstly, when they're sewing you up after the episiotomy, suggest that they just keep on sewing. You won't want anything going *in* or coming *out* of there ever again. And approach the 'Super Mum' myth with the same attitude we developed in 1991 towards official war reports on 'friendly fire' and 'collateral damage'.

Read between the lies.

TARIQ ALI

1992

Behind the Boundary

Wasim and Wakar triumphant

Photo: Tony Harris/Press Association

IN 1992 I became a born-again cricketing enthusiast. The occasion was provided by the Pakistan versus England test series, but the person responsible for my re-conversion was Chengiz, my nine-year-old son. A subscriber to *Wisden* for the last two years, an eagle-eyed devotee of first-class cricket scores, an avid student of cricket history, this boy has become a living encyclopaedia of the sport. For over a year now a large poster of the Pakistani fast bowler Waqar Younis has adorned his bedroom wall.

Chengiz speaks of fifties' cricketing heroes with a knowledge that brings back my own childhood memories. When I tell him that I saw Sobers and the three Ws – Weekes, Worrell and Walcott – play in a West Indies versus Pakistan test match in Lahore, he is incredulous, questioning me in some detail and challenging some of my improvisations. I may have witnessed the encounter, but it is he who remembers the scores. When his mother has the gall to admit that she has never heard of Len Hutton, Jim Laker, Don Bradman or Hanif Mohammed, a scornful and pitying look lights his face. What do they know of this world, who do not cricket know?

There is something wonderfully anachronistic about a sport which gives itself five days to decide a contest. Hardly a prison of measured time. And so it happened that on a beautiful summer's day, with the Third Test evenly balanced on the fourth day, Chengiz and I traipsed off to Lord's. He was anxious to buy an official Pakistan sweat-shirt and sit as close to the official supporters as possible. He was disappointed on both counts. The sweat-shirts were too big and our seats in the Edrich stand were in the same row as a claque of champagne-swilling yuppies under the leadership of a loquacious Chinese accountant.

What separated us from them was the solitary figure of a man in his early thirties, slightly over-dressed for the day and the occasion. He wore a heavy, brown tweed suit, a matching tweed hat and a woollen waist-coat. His Sony, tuned permanently to Radio 3, was plugged firmly to his ears. His lap was loaded with a pile of cricket magazines and reference books. When all this proved futile and he still couldn't understand why the yuppies were cheering and Chengiz seemed upset, he would unplug himself and ask me to explain. It was on the first of these occasions that I realized he was a German. It soon emerged that he was a non-playing member of the Hamburg Cricket Club. His interest in the game was 'theoretical'. The sun was strong. Even a glimpse of the tweed suit made me sweat. It was a bit like feeling itchy at the memory of being assailed by mosquitos in the tropics. His questions began to irritate me. I wanted to bring our acquaintanceship to an end. I suggested that in order to really understand what was going on he should forget *Wisden* and study Hegel's *Science of Logic.*

'Hegel?' he asked in amazement. 'Hegel! What has he to do with cricket?'

I warmed to him slightly. At least he recognized the name. I explained that the late and great West Indian historian C. L. R. James had argued that Hegel's work could be used to understand and analyse any development in society. Furthermore, I pointed out that the links between left-Hegelianism and cricket had inspired a number of works, some of which were not yet published. I expressed shock that a German cricket club could ignore such an obvious connection. I insisted that he read James's classic *Beyond the Boundary.* The aficionado from Hamburg was singularly unimpressed. He looked at me as if I were unhinged. For the rest of the day he directed his questions at Chengiz.

As the game proceeded Chengiz was in good spirits. His eyes were shining as he stood and cheered the fall of every English wicket. Waqar Younis and Wasim Akram were bowling in tandem. What a wonderful sight it was. These two young Pakistani bowlers employed pace and swing with such beauty and skill as to be virtually unplayable, beating the bat with outswingers and, occasionally, with late inswing. When either of them tired, the plump leg-spinner Mushtaq Ahmed was brought on to vary the attack, which he did with unconcealed glee as his googlies struck home. England were bowled out in their second innings for 175 runs. Pakistan needed 141 to win the test. The yuppies drowned their sorrow in yet more champagne. Their crestfallen but unsentimental leader went down to the betting shop. I wondered whether he was going to put money on a Pakistani victory. Our friend from Hamburg finally removed his jacket.

I had not been to a test match since 1962 and that had been in Lahore. Imtiaz Ahmed had scored a scintillating 50 in forty minutes against an MCC A team. Pakistani cricket in the fifties and early sixties was very much a game dominated by 'gentlemen'. The cricket team, like the country itself, was carved out of a larger Indian entity. A. H. Kardar and Fazal Mahmood, who were captain and deputy in the fifties, had gained their skills prior to Independence and Partition in 1947. Hanif Mohammed and his brothers were a post-colonial discovery and the combination worked well. When Fazal Mahmood took six wickets apiece in the two innings against England at the Oval in 1954, Pakistan had won its first test match against England. Fazal became an overnight hero. But very little cricket was played in those years and once the Kardar generation passed the forty-year mark, the game went into decline.

From the age of eight till my early teens, I used to love playing cricket. I created a team of street urchins, clothed them from my own wardrobe and challenged neighbouring teams. The bulk of my team never went to school and, often, sitting in my classroom being bored out of my skull, I used to dream of those free souls playing cricket in the *maidan*. Sometimes I used to skip classes and join my team for the day, making sure I was back at school when the car came to collect me. These idylls were brought to an end when my truancy was discovered and punished.

Later, at Government College, Lahore, some good friends were in the college team and I made sure I was always present at the annual fixture against Islamia College, a great cricketing event of the city. A number of my friends later became test players, but by then I was no longer in Pakistan.

In Oxford during the mid-sixties I had become disinterested in cricket. I never went to a match locally and while I followed the political situation in Pakistan very closely, I lost all contact with Pakistani cricket. In 1968 two of my old college friends from Pakistan were part of the test team playing Britain. They rang, left messages, offered free tickets, demanded some support, but I declined all their inducements. I was so immersed in radical politics and the anti-Vietnam war campaigns that there was very little time for anything else.

As the revolutionary wave subsided, cricket slowly re-entered my consciousness, but not with the same fervour. C. L. R. James taught that politics and cricket were not incompatible and, of course, he was right, but the old interest never returned. I would often irritate friends by refusing to take sides in any test. During the seventies I became a closet West Indian supporter, but even then I rarely watched an entire test on television and never switched on to Radio 3.

Slowly, as my own political activism declined and I became immersed in writing and film-making, my interest in cricket began to return. By now the game had become incredibly commercialized and my interest might well have waned had it not been for Chengiz. I thought about all this as I watched the Lord's test. C. L. R. James had, in relation to the West Indies, written of cricket as 'a means of national expression'. Despite the transformation of the game, despite the Packer circus and one-day cricket and the World Cup, the game still reflected certain national characteristics. The Pakistan team had been changed beyond recognition. Cricket was now played everywhere in Pakistan. Imran Khan described the history of Pakistani cricket as a *mélange* of nepotism, inefficiency, corruption, constant bickering and indiscipline. Very true. And yet, Imran had succeeded, against the odds, in taking on the cricketing establishment and ensuring that merit played some part in selecting a team. Waqar Younis, Wasim Akram, Mushtaq Ahmed and Inzamam-ul-Haq were the fruits of Imran Khan's long years of captaincy and public polemics against the cricket-bureaucrats in Pakistan.

The clashes between England and Pakistan in previous years had become legendary: two competing petty-bourgeois nationalisms locked in conflict on the cricket field. Nineteen ninety-two was no exception. A badly out-of-form empire-loyalist, Ian Botham, wanted to take on the brilliant but erratic Javed Miandad (a supporter of the neo-fascist MQM in Karachi – a political party which specialized in exaggerating a variety of small but real grievances into mountains of imagined oppressions). Deprived of Imran Khan, the Pakistanis hired a PR firm, but most of the tabloids were unimpressed.

Pakistani cricket had cast off its colonial mask. It had become the only effective vehicle for Pakistani nationalism. During General Zia's dictatorship, cricket in Pakistan had a function not unlike that of circuses in ancient Rome. After the restoration of democracy it had become one of the few things that gave ordinary citizens a sense of pride and achievement, albeit by proxy. The cumulative impact was to make every ten-year-old boy dream of glories on the cricket field. Imran Khan, in particular, as a captain and a cricketer, fighting simultaneously on two fronts – the cricket field and the intrigue and backbiting which took place behind closed doors – was greatly admired. It was the strength of this example that inspired Wasim Akram, Waqar Younis and Inzamam-ul-Haq to start taking cricket seriously.

Cricket, like the Permanent Settlement Act of Bengal, had been brought to the sub-continent by the British. It was first, like the English language itself, confined to the colonizers. Then it was carefully extended to the indigenous élites. Slowly the middle-classes began to acquire an interest in the game, apart from the odd servant boy whose genius could not be overlooked by his masters. After two decades of independence the old bondage was loosened. By the end of the eighties and the nineties, Pakistani and Indian cricket had come into its own. It had taken over a century and a half for the sport to descend from the top of the social pyramid and embrace the whole of society. Javed Miandad was one of the results of this change. A bad captain, awful politics, but a brilliant batsman, reminding one of John Arlott's poetic tribute to another great batsman:

> *So, in timed swoop, he moves to charm.*
> *The ball down-swirling from the bowler's arm*
> *Along some glissade of his own creation,*
> *Beyond the figures' black and white rotation.*

English cricket had, in contrast, travelled in the opposite direction. In *Beyond the Boundary*, C. L. R. James invoked the majestic past of English cricket. He challenged the view that cricket was the child of Victoriana, arguing that the essential features of the game were formed between 1778 and 1830:

It was created by the yeoman farmer, the gamekeeper, the potter, the tinker, the Nottingham coal-miner, the Yorkshire factory hand. These artisans made it, men of hand and eye. Rich and idle young noblemen and some substantial city people contributed money, organisation and prestige. Between them, by 1837, they had evolved a highly complicated game with all the typical characteristics of a national art form: founded on elements long present in the nation, profoundly popular in origin, yet attracting to it disinterested elements of the leisured and educated classes . . . There was nothing in the slightest degree Victorian about it.

During the Victorian period, the needs of the Empire became paramount. Imperialism embraced every feature of British life, including cricket. Much has changed, of course, but the legacy is still present. The word 'imperial' may have fallen into disuse, but the international centre of cricket is still London. The MCC still dominates the International Cricket Conference and the MCC itself is controlled by a generation which has fond memories of the old colonial past. One reason for this domination is that the Americans don't play cricket, but this is a meagre consolation for the new practitioners of the sport from the old colonies.

The fact is that English cricket has, with a few exceptions, become incredibly mediocre. In the old days the Empire had given the cricket field a sense of purpose: 'playing the game' in the fashion of an Englishman. Cricket was a means of culturally assimilating the colonials, whether they be black, brown or white.

It was all different now. Britain was in decline. Its manufacturing industry had been devastated by the self-proclaimed Thatcher 'revolution'. An electorate bribed by North Sea oil revenues and encouraged to believe that victory in the Falklands war was a reversal of the decline. The basest instincts possible were encouraged by the *Sun* and a new brand of academic columnists in *The Times*. Hardly surprising that this mood was reflected both on the field and in the stands. One could take the analogy further. Is it too far-fetched to see similarities between the tired, stale, uninspiring managers of English cricket and their equivalents in the Tory Cabinet?

The sad fact was that in cricket the decline was only too obvious (as it now is in virtually every other field of public and private endeavour), but few wanted to believe that this was the case. The West Indies fast bowlers were too fast. So the rules were changed, restricting the number of bouncers that could be bowled in one over. Wasim and Waqar were taking too many wickets. It must be because they tampered with the ball. Pakistani umpires cheated. British umpires made mistakes. When Imran campaigned for neutral umpires his arguments were politely ignored. If the Indian spinners were unplayable it was because the pitches were specially prepared for them. When all arguments failed it was easy to attack the country in question. Pakistan was awful (no booze, no bars and no groupies); India was polluted. The West Indies is fine, not least because the Western-owned tourist industries are reducing the local population to the status of virtual slaves. Hotel empires are the new plantations. Forgive this lengthy digression. Back to Lord's. Something awful is happening. Having bowled England out for 175 runs in their second innings, Pakistan need 141 to win the match. Chris Lewis is roaring down to bowl again. Some English enthusiasts, forgetting that Lewis is black, are chanting, 'Come on, you Whites,' oblivious to irony. Three Pakistani batsmen, including Captain Miandad, have been dismissed by him for a duck. Typical, I think to myself. They think it's too easy. All the concentration has gone.

The yuppies are on their feet, stinking of alcohol and cheering. Suddenly their leader falls back on his chair, his head in his hands. He turns to me and complains:

'What's happened. Miandad is the greatest batsman in the world. Why is he out?'

This anguish is in marked contrast to his raucous behaviour. He confesses that he had only a few hours ago placed a bet. A hundred pounds on Miandad reaching 50 today. I couldn't help laughing at the contradictions of the English cricket fan. For some reason he reminded me of the people who wanted to vote Labour, but whose greed had placed the cross alongside the wrong name in the polling booth . . .

My friend from Hamburg is looking sympathetically at Chengiz, whose grief is very visible. Knowing my son well I ask him whether we should leave and see the rest on TV. He shakes his head. Then Inzamam is run out thanks to a stupid call from Aamir Sohail. I can almost hear him muttering 'Motherfucker' as he passes his partner on the way back to the pavilion. Now it is

Wasim Akram's turn to bat. He does so with care and caution. Chengiz remarks that Wasim Akram should be the captain. I agree. More wickets fall and it seems as if we've lost. Not wanting to witness the scenes of jubilation, Chengiz suggests we leave just as Waqar Younis is coming in to bat at number eight. In the Pakistani balcony we can see the last man, Aqib Javed, padded up and looking miserable.

An hour later Wasim and Waqar were still at the crease and Pakistan had won. Chengiz looked at me mournfully. He wished we'd stayed on. Cricket, despite everything, was still as gloriously unpredictable as ever.

*A Note
on the
Contributors*

TARIQ ALI

Tariq Ali was born in Lahore (then India and now Pakistan) in 1943 and was educated at Punjab University and Exeter College, Oxford. He is the author of over a dozen books on history, world politics and biography, including *The Nehrus and the Gandhis*, *Can Pakistan Survive?* and *Streetfighting Years: An Autobiography of the Sixties*. With Howard Brenton, he has written two highly acclaimed plays, *Iranian Nights* and *Moscow Gold*. He has also written two novels, *Redemption* and *Shadows of the Pomegranate Tree*.

Tariq Ali produced *The Bandung File* for four years and is currently the producer of the arts series, *Rear Window*, on Channel 4.

He lives in London.

Photo: Alan Titmuss

JULIAN BARNES

Julian Barnes was born in Leicester in 1946.

He is the author of seven novels: *Metroland*, *Before She Met Me*, *Flaubert's Parrot*, *Staring at the Sun*, *A History of the World in 10½ Chapters*, *Talking It Over* and *The Porcupine*.

His novels have won many prizes throughout the world; in France he has won the *Prix Médicis* and the *Prix Fémina*, and was made a *Chevalier de l'Ordre des Arts et des Lettres* in 1988. He was awarded the Shakespeare Prize by the FVS Foundation of Hamburg in 1993.

He lives in London.

Photo: Gerry Bauer

JIM CRACE

Jim Crace was born in 1946 and brought up in north London. He worked as a freelance journalist, writing for the *Sunday Telegraph*, the *TLS*, the *Sunday Times* and *Radio Times*. He is the author of *Continent*, which won the 1986 *Guardian* Fiction Prize, Whitbread First Novel Prize and David Higham Prize, *The Gift of Stones*, and *Arcadia*. He lives in Birmingham with his wife and two children.

RUSSELL HOBAN

Born in 1925 in Pennsylvania, Russell Hoban was an illustrator before becoming a writer. He has written many books for children and his adult novels are *The Lion of Boaz-Jachin and Jachin-Boaz*, *Kleinzeit*, *Turtle Diary*, *Riddley Walker*, *Pilgermann* and *The Medusa Frequency*. He has lived in London since 1969 and is currently collaborating with Harrison Birtwistle on an opera.

CHRISTOPHER HOPE

Christopher Hope was born in Johannesburg. He has published five novels: *A Separate Development* (winner of the 1981 David Higham Prize for fiction), *Kruger's Alp* (winner of the 1985 Whitbread Prize for Fiction), *The Hottentot Room*, *My Chocolate Redeemer*, *Serenity House* (shortlisted for the 1992 Booker Prize) and two works of non-fiction: *White Boy Running*, winner of the CNA Literary Award in South Africa, and *Moscow! Moscow!*.

CLIVE JAMES

Clive James was born in Sydney in 1939. He appears regularly on BBC television and is the author of more than twenty books. As well as three volumes of autobiography, *Unreliable Memoirs*, *Falling Towards England* and *May Week Was in June*, he has published collections of criticism, verse and travel writing. His most recent novel was *Brrm! Brrm!* In 1992 he was awarded the Order of Australia.

TAMA JANOWITZ

Tama Janowitz was born in 1959 in San Francisco, the daughter of a poet and a psychiatrist. During the course of her life, she has moved house almost forty times. She attended Barnard College and received an MA in fiction from Hollins College. She studied playwriting at the Yale School of Drama, was a fellow in fiction writing at the Fine Arts Work Center in Provincetown, Massachusetts, and obtained an MFA in writing from Columbia University. After receiving a National Endowment for the Arts Award for fiction, she moved to Manhattan. A number of her stories, written between 1979 and 1986, made up the best-selling collection *Slaves of New York*. Her first novel, *American Dad*, was published when Tama Janowitz was 22 years old.

Andy Warhol had bought the screen rights to *Slaves of New York*. Following his death, the collection was filmed by Merchant Ivory and released in 1989.

Tama Janowitz lives in New York City with her British husband, Tim Hunt, and her two dogs.

Photo: David Modell

MARK LAWSON

Mark Lawson was born in London in 1962.

His first job in journalism was with the *Universe*, a weekly Catholic newspaper, and he subsequently worked for *The Times* and the *Sunday Times* before joining the *Independent* in 1986 as TV critic and then parliamentary sketchwriter. Since 1988 he has been chief feature writer for the *Independent Magazine* and he was TV critic of the *Independent on Sunday* from 1990 to 1991. He writes a weekly column on arts and politics for the *Independent*. He won a British Press Award in 1987; BP Arts Journalism Awards in 1989, 1990 and 1991; and Broadcast Journalism Awards in 1989 (critic) and 1990 (feature writer).

He has written and presented two television documentaries and one television play: *Byline – Vote for Ron* (BBC, 1989), *J'Accuse – Coronation Street* (Channel 4, 1991) and *The Vision Thing* (BBC, 1993). He appears regularly on television and radio magazine programmes.

His first work of fiction was *Bloody Margaret: Three Political Fantasies*, which was shortlisted for various prizes including the *Sunday Times* Young Writer of the Year Award and the First Book section of the Commonwealth Writers' Prize. He recently published his first book of non-fiction, *The Battle for Room Service: Journeys to All the Safe Places*, and is currently writing a novel.

He lives in London with his wife and son.

Photo: Jillian Edelstein

KATHY LETTE

Kathy Lette was born in Sylvania Waters. She is regarded as a national treasure and her outrageous views on men, relationships and the rigours of modern life are frequently sought on radio and TV. Her reputation as an *enfant terrible* was established when she fled school at sixteen and formed the Salami Sisters, an irreverent cabaret duo.

Her diverse career includes stints as a satirical reporter on Australian TV, a columnist for the *Sydney Morning Herald* and a comedy writer for Columbia Pictures in California. Since moving to London in 1989 she has presented Thames TV's *O1 For London* and BBC's *Behind the Headlines*. Her first novel, *Puberty Blues*, leapt straight on to the national bestseller list in 1979 and was subsequently adapted for cinema. Her collection of short stories, *Girl's Night Out*, was a bestseller in Britain and Australia and will shortly be made into a film. Her second novel, *The Llama Parlour*, even managed to cheer up Salman Rushdie. Her latest novel, *Foetal Attraction*, will be published as a Picador hardback in 1993. She lives in London with her husband and two children.

NORMAN LEWIS

Norman Lewis was born in London. He has written thirteen novels and nine non-fiction works. *A Dragon Apparent* and *Golden Earth* are considered classics of travel, and *Naples '44* has been described as one of the ten outstanding books about the Second World War. He relaxes by his travels to off-beat parts of the world, which he prefers to be as remote as possible; otherwise he lives with his family in introspective, almost monastic, calm in the depths of Essex.

Photo: Paul Pringle

PATRICK McCABE

Patrick McCabe was born in County Monaghan, Ireland, in 1955.

In 1979 he received the Hennessy Award for a short story, and has had short stories published in *Panurge*, the *Irish Times*, the *Cork Examiner*, and other magazines. Two of his short stories were broadcast on RTE, in Ireland, and several plays were broadcast by the BBC and RTE.

He has published a children's story, *The Adventures of Shay Mouse*, and three novels, *Music on Clinton Street*, *Carn* and *The Butcher Boy*, which won the *Irish Times*/Aer Lingus Literature Prize for Fiction and was shortlisted for the 1992 Booker Prize. His play *Frank Pig Says Hello*, based on *The Butcher Boy*, has been performed in Dublin, London and Glasgow. In 1991 he was awarded a bursary from the Arts Council of Ireland.

He lives in London with his wife and two daughters, where he currently teaches.

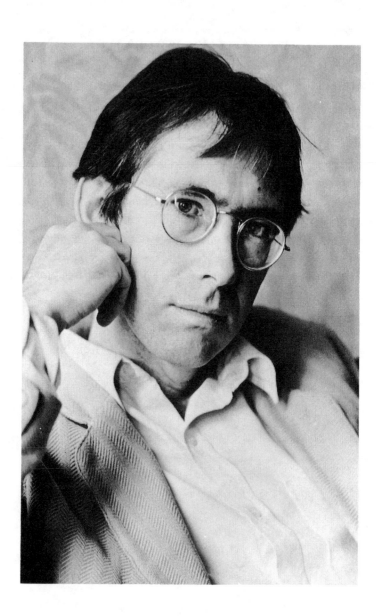

IAN McEWAN

Ian McEwan was born in 1948 and spent much of his childhood moving around the world with his father's military postings. He studied at Sussex and East Anglia.

He has written two collections of short stories – *First Love, Last Rites* and *In Between the Sheets* – and five novels: *The Cement Garden*, *The Comfort of Strangers*, *The Child in Time*, *The Innocent*, and *Black Dogs*. He has also written several television plays, including *Solid Geometry* and *The Imitation Game*, and the libretto for Michael Berkeley's oratorio *Or Shall We Die?*.

ROBERT McLIAM WILSON

Robert McLiam Wilson was born in Belfast in 1964. He read English at Cambridge, but left university early to write his first novel, *Ripley Bogle*, which was published in 1989. It won the Rooney Prize, the Betty Trask Prize, the Hughes Award and the Irish Book Award. His second novel, *Manfred's Pain*, was shortlisted for the Whitbread Prize for Fiction 1992.

He is the author of *The Dispossessed* with Donovan Wylie, a non-fiction work about poverty.

He has also made a number of documentary films including *The Beginner's Guide to the State We're In* in 1993.

CANDIA McWILLIAM

Candia McWilliam was born in 1955 in Edinburgh where she was educated until, at the age of thirteen, she went to school in England and then to Girton College, Cambridge.

She is the author of *A Case of Knives*, which was the joint winner of the 1988 Betty Trask Award, and *A Little Stranger*.

She has a son and daughter by her first marriage and a son by her second. She lives in Oxford.

CHARLES NICHOLL

Charles Nicholl was born in London in 1950. He studied English at Cambridge, and in 1972 won the *Telegraph Magazine* Young Writer of the Year Award. As well as contributing to all the major national newspapers and magazines he has written two travel books, *The Fruit Palace* and *Borderlines*; a study of Elizabethan alchemy, *The Chemical Theatre*; and a biography of the pamphleteer Thomas Nashe, *A Cup of News*. *The Reckoning*, the first full-length investigation of the killing of Christopher Marlowe, was published in 1992 and won the James Tait Black Memorial Prize. His current project – a reconstruction of Sir Walter Raleigh's journey in search of El Dorado – was the subject of a recent Channel 4 film.

CARYL PHILLIPS

Caryl Phillips was born in 1958 in St Kitts, West Indies, and came with his family to England in the same year. He was brought up in Leeds and educated at Oxford, where he read English at The Queen's College.

He has written numerous scripts for film, theatre, radio and television including the film *Playing Away*. He is the author of *The Final Passage*, *A State of Independence*, *The European Tribe* (which won the 1987 Martin Luther King Memorial Prize) and *Higher Ground*.

In 1992 he won the *Sunday Times* Young Writer of the Year Award for his novel *Cambridge*. In 1993 his fifth novel, *Crossing the River*, was published.

As well as lecturing in Stockholm and Germany, he has taught in Ghana and is currently Professor of English at Amherst College, Massachusetts.

271

Photo: Douglas Brothers

DAVID PROFUMO

David Profumo was born in London in 1955 and educated at the universities of Oxford and London. A former teacher and Deputy Editor of the *Fiction Magazine*, he is now a freelance writer and a columnist with the *Daily Telegraph*. His first novel, *Sea Music*, was awarded the Geoffrey Faber Memorial Prize in 1989, and he co-edited (with Graham Swift) *The Magic Wheel: An Anthology of Fishing in Literature*. His second novel, *The Weather in Iceland*, was published by Picador in 1993.

OLIVER SACKS

Oliver Sacks was born in London in 1933 and educated at St Paul's School, The Queen's College, Oxford, and the Middlesex Hospital, prior to further work and training in the United States. Following a period of research in neurochemistry and neuropathology he returned to clinical work, interesting himself particularly in migraine (the subject of his first book), and the care of post-encephalitic patients described in *Awakenings*. He is also the author of *A Leg to Stand On*, *The Man Who Mistook His Wife for a Hat* and *Seeing Voices*. Dr Sacks is Clinical Professor of Neurology at the Albert Einstein College of Medicine and Consultant Neurologist for Beth Abraham Hospital and Little Sisters of the Poor, in New York.

GRAHAM SWIFT

Graham Swift was born in London in 1949. His stories first
appeared in *London Magazine*. He is the author of five novels:
The Sweet Shop Owner, *Shuttlecock*, which received the Geoffrey Faber Memorial Prize, the internationally acclaimed
Waterland, which was shortlisted for the Booker prize and
won the *Guardian* Fiction Award, the Winifred Holtby Memorial Prize and the Italian Premio Grinzane Cavour, *Out of
This World* and *Ever After*. He has published a collection of
short stories, *Learning to Swim*, and co-edited (with David
Profumo) *The Magic Wheel: An Anthology of Fishing in
Literature*.

COLM TÓIBÍN

Colm Tóibín was born in Ireland in 1955 and now lives in Dublin. He is the author of two non-fiction books, *Walking Along the Border* and *Homage to Barcelona*. His first novel, *The South*, was winner of the *Irish Times*/Aer Lingus Literature Prize 1991, and his second novel, *The Heather Blazing*, won the Encore Award in 1993.

EDMUND WHITE

Edmund White was born in Cincinnati, Ohio, in 1940. He has been a teacher of writing at Columbia University and Executive Director of the New York Institute of the Humanities. His books include *A Boy's Own Story*, *The Beautiful Room is Empty*, *Caracole*, *Nocturnes for the King of Naples*, *Forgetting Elena*, *States of Desire: Travels in Gay America* and *Genet*.

In 1993 he was made a *Chevalier de l'Ordre des Arts et des Lettres*.

He lives in Paris.